Foreign Affairs 1815-1865

Collins New Advanced History Series

Foreign Affairs 1815-1865

D R Ward

Collins London and Glasgow

General Editors
K H Randell   J W Hunt
© D R Ward 1972

Printed in Great Britain
Collins Clear-Type Press
Set in Monotype Plantin

ISBN 0 00 327211 7

First published 1972
Third impression 1977

Cover illustration: National Army Museum

Contents

Editors' foreword

The series of which this book is a part is designed to meet the needs of students in Sixth Forms and those taking courses in further and higher education. In assessing these needs two factors especially have been taken into account: the limits on the students' time which preclude the reading of all the important scholarly works, and the importance of providing stimulus to thought and imagination. Therefore the series, which has considerably more space available than even the larger single-volume textbooks on the period, presents the interpretations which have altered or increased our understanding of the age, as well as including sufficient detail to illustrate and enliven the subject. Most important of all, emphasis has been placed on discussion. Instead of outlining supposedly established facts, problems are posed as they were faced by the people of the time and as they confront the historian today in his task of interpretation. The student is thus enabled to approach the subject in an attitude of enquiry, and is encouraged to exercise his own mind on the arguments, never closed, of historiography. In so doing he will gain some knowledge of the methods of historians and of the kinds of evidence they use. He should also find enjoyment by the way.

The arrangement of the series, with several volumes covering particular aspects over a long period, and others with more strict chronological limits, has enabled each author to concentrate on an area of special interest, and should make for flexibility in use by the reader.

K.H.R.
J.W.M.

Full details of historical works referred to in the text will be found in the list of Further Reading on page 123. Only where the work is not included is a full reference given in the text.

Chapter I

The character of the period

1 From war to peace The year 1815 saw the final defeat of Napoleon and the end of the war which had plagued Europe, with only brief respites, since 1792. The change from chronic war to comparative tranquility is a convenient point at which to begin a period of historical study, especially as international relations in the half-century which followed were deeply coloured by the peace settlement, usually described as the Vienna settlement, which was concluded in 1815. Despite its popularity, however, 1815 as a starting point does have disadvantages.

First, the peace can assume too much significance; it can be praised or blamed for all that happened or failed to happen in subsequent years. This misconception lies at the root of most of the extreme judgements of the Vienna settlement, whether they castigate it for lack of vision—especially with regard to the forces of nationalism and liberalism—and attack its cynical disinterest in the wishes of the people who lived in the territories whose future it decided, or whether they extol it as the principal cause of forty years of European peace.

A second danger in seeing 1815 as the beginning of a new historical period is the failure to understand the nature of the conflict which preceded it. It is possible, for example, to forget that the war which ended in 1815 had been fought against France as well as against Napoleon and the forces of revolution. Long before 1815 these had become aspects of the same conflict, but they differed in the relative emphasis accorded to them by the various combatants. Britain, for instance, the most consistent of the allies in opposition to France, was certainly opposing the principles enunciated in the Revolution, particularly in its most extreme phase. Nevertheless, it is fair to say that fear of revolutionary doctrines was the least significant of the reasons for the British government's determination to defeat France. The chief motive was to frustrate the threat of European dominance posed by revolutionary France in the garb of a crusader for liberty. English fears had become more pronounced with the rise to power of Napoleon, and the conviction had grown that so long as Napoleon remained her ruler, France would strive to dominate Europe; any compromise she accepted would only be a tactical withdrawal. Hence Britain's aim was both to unseat Napoleon and to confine France within her traditional frontiers. Britain had been fighting Napoleon overseas, however, as well as in Europe. The Revolutionary and Napoleonic Wars marked a further stage in the Franco-British colonial rivalry of the eighteenth century, and 1815 was the culmination of a long period of British success. It was in this context that Britain attacked the colonies of Holland, as ally and client of the French. Britain fought Napoleon not only as the heir of the Revolution, but as the heir of Colbert and Louis XIV. The different strands of British hostility to France were drawn together by Napoleon's expedition to Egypt in 1798: the general of the Revolution at the same time demonstrated his own grandiose schemes of personal domination and reopened an eighteenth-century conflict by rousing British fears for India.

Austria on the other hand, an autocracy like Russia and Prussia, felt herself much more threatened by revolutionary ideology than did Britain. The belief in the sovereignty of the people, signified in France by the change, early in the Revolution, of Louis XVI's title from King of France to King of the French, meant danger for an empire like the Austrian where there were no distinctively Austrian people. Instead the state was founded on the dynastic ownership of land, the people who lived on the land being the subjects of the monarchy; they were drawn from different races, spoke different languages and even followed different religions.

Because the allies were, to some extent, in conflict with different features of an ascendant France their attitudes to a defeated France would also differ. Undue emphasis upon the confrontation between France and the victorious allies—Austria, Britain, Prussia and Russia—can mask the other rivalries and quarrels between European powers which had continued to exercise the minds of statesmen during the war with France and were to play an important part in the peace settlement and to persist after 1815. In the early nineteenth century the Prussian military writer von Clausewitz claimed: 'War is nothing more than the continuation of politics by other means.' Although an examination of the peace of 1815 is a useful point of departure for a study of British foreign policy, it is essential that the settlement should be seen in the light of the Revolutionary and Napoleonic Wars, which had forcibly illustrated the objectives of the various powers.

Although the victors differed somewhat in their concept of the peace settlement, they shared a common desire that France and Napoleon should not threaten their security again. Essential to Napoleon's downfall had been the alliance which had held his enemies together in the final stages of the war, and this alliance became the guarantee against renewed French aggression. For some time, Castlereagh had envisaged the co-operation necessary to defeat France as lasting beyond the war itself to preserve the peace. In the Cabinet instructions which he wrote for himself in 1813, based on the ideas of William Pitt, he affirmed: 'The Treaty of Alliance is not to terminate with the war, but to contain defensive engagements, with mutual obligations to support the Powers attacked by France, with a certain extent of stipulated succours.' The concept was embodied in the Quadruple Alliance, largely the work of Castlereagh, which was signed at Chaumont in March 1814 and bound the allies to maintain the alliance for twenty years after the end of the war and help one another in the event of French interference with a future peace settlement. This alliance, renewed on Napoleon's return from Elba and then again in November 1815, when the second Peace of Paris was signed with France, stipulated that the return to power in France of Napoleon, or any of his family, would entail a resumption of war.

Security against France, however, depended upon more than an alliance; the future shape of Europe was clearly important. Various agreements had already been concluded before the First Peace of Paris in 1814, but the critical decisions depended upon strenuous negotiations at the Congress of Vienna which were not completed until the summer of 1815. In an attempt to protect Europe from attack by France the states on her frontiers were strengthened. Most of the Rhineland went to Prussia, and the Austrian Netherlands were joined to the new Kingdom of Holland, which, it was hoped, would create a more stable situation in that vital area. This latter solution was particularly favoured by England because it kept the control of the important River Scheldt out of the hands of any major power. The German Confederation was designed to make French diplomatic interference with the smaller German states more difficult, at least so long as Austria and Prussia supported one another. The Austrian Chancellor Metternich's wish for an Italian federation under Austrian protection was not granted, but Sardinia-Piedmont was enlarged, and Austria sought to establish herself firmly in the peninsula, both through her direct rule in Lombardy and Venetia in the north, and further south through the Pope and several client princelings.

Strengthening France's neighbours would make any future aggression more difficult, but an important contribution to the prevention of future wars would be to lessen French bellicosity. 'Security and not revenge' was how Castlereagh phrased his view of the proper objective of the allies in 1814. Thus he opposed schemes for a punitive peace since, he argued, a humiliated and embittered France would have to be held down for the foreseeable future and would have no inducement to accept the status quo. With Napoleon's return from exile in Elba in 1815 and his attempt to reverse his defeat with a new descent upon the Low Countries, the arguments for a severe peace were greatly strengthened.

Nevertheless, Castlereagh's view triumphed over that of the Prussians, who wished to punish France. The Second Peace of Paris, signed with the restored Bourbon King of France in November 1815, was only a little less lenient than the peace of the previous year. France lost a few frontier districts but retained the boundaries of 1792, the year when war had first broken out. She had to accept and defray the expenses of an army of occupation under the command of the Duke of Wellington. Besides the payment of an indemnity, France was forced to agree to the restoration to their former owners of Napoleon's enormous collection of looted art treasures. These changes were really the least that could be exacted after the events of the Hundred Days.

A further reason for moderation was the realisation that a harsh peace would create among the French people resentment against the government which had negotiated it. Once the allies had decided in 1815 upon another attempt to restore the Bourbons to the French throne it became important not to add to the difficulties in the way of a successful restoration. Talleyrand, the French Foreign Minister, had claimed that the peace settlement was based upon the principle of legitimacy, and if this was so, a Bourbon restoration would naturally have been foreseen. In fact, the principle of legitimacy was only adhered to when it suited the allies, and otherwise ignored; witness the handing over to Austria of the former Venetian Republic. The Bourbon restoration was, in reality, far from assured, and resulted partly from the difficulty of finding any other solution which did not seem to favour one of the allies at the expense of the others.

Although Castlereagh urged that 'it is not our business to collect trophies, but to try, if we can, to bring the world back to peaceful habits', the peace was also used by the major powers as a chance for reciprocal compensation for their efforts in the war. Thus Prussia's gains in the Rhineland and Austria's absorption of the former Venetian Republic were the result of self-aggrandisement as well as part of a scheme for the protection of Europe. It was over compensation that most difficulties arose, because of fears that one Power might gain more than another; fears that were exacerbated by old rivalries and jealousies.

Perhaps the most significant were the jealousies and ambitions of the three Eastern Courts—Russia, Austria and Prussia. In the late eighteenth century Russia's emergence as a major power and her expansion west and south had brought her increasingly into competition with the Austrian Empire. Most of all the two empires found themselves opposed in the south of Europe, where Russia was advancing into the territories once held by the Turks. It was this rivalry and the fear of what it might lead to that had prompted Frederick the Great's initiative in the first partition of Poland in 1772, which was an attempt to divert Austrian and Russian interests and at the same time allow Prussia to share in the spoils. The subsequent partitions of 1793 and 1795, which removed Poland from the map, had maintained tension in the area. Napoleon had created the Grand Duchy of Warsaw with Polish lands torn from the defeated Prussia and Austria, but his defeat reopened the question of Poland's future and of the rival shares that Austria, Prussia and Russia might expect. The Russian Tsar, Alexander I, wished to create a new Polish kingdom with himself as king, and to reward Prussia for waiving what had been her share by giving her Saxony. The other powers resisted so bitterly that the division enabled France to split her conquerors and even take part in a secret alliance with Britain and Austria against the Russian proposals. This determined resistance was due to their fear that the acquisition of Saxony by Prussia and of all Poland by Russia would alter the balance of European power. In the event the dispute was settled without violence, with Prussia retaining some of Poland but receiving only two-fifths of Saxony.

The personality of the Tsar was of major importance in the arguments over Poland as it was throughout the period of the peace settlement. By no means always consistent, the Tsar is a baffling figure: 'Too weak for ambition, but too strong for pure vanity', as Metternich described him. What stands out even above his intelligence is his pride. To him the shape and the nature of the Europe which emerged from Napoleon's defeat would be less important than his own part in moulding it. Very often his schemes were idealistic, as seen in his desire to create a new

Poland which would enjoy a constitution, but usually they were conditioned by self-interest—witness his desire to be king of the new Poland. Once the French invasion of Russia had been repulsed, he saw the defeat of Napoleon and the movement of Russian armies through Germany and into France as presenting enormous opportunities for the expansion of his country and the increase of his personal power. His countrymen, not interested in the Tsar's individual supremacy, preferred further penetration into the Turkish Empire and regarded involvement in Germany and western Europe as irrelevant to Russian interests. This division is partly explained by and partly explains the large proportion of Alexander's advisers who were themselves foreigners; Pozzo di Borgo, Nesselrode, La Harpe, Stein and Capo d'Istria were all at one time or another influential in shaping Russian policy, and none of them was Russian.

Perhaps the best known product of the Tsar's personal initiative in the diplomacy of this period was the Holy Alliance. Sometimes confused with the Quadruple Alliance, with which it had nothing whatever to do, the Holy Alliance was signed in September 1815 by the sovereigns of Russia, Austria and Prussia, with other rulers invited to sign subsequently. In the event, with the exception of the Pope and the Prince Regent, the Christian kings of Europe signed, agreeing that 'the course which the relations of powers had assumed, must be replaced by an order of things founded on the exalted truth of the eternal [Christian] religion'. Although it has sometimes been argued that the Alliance was an attempt by the Tsar to isolate his country's enemy, Turkey, it seems much more likely that his appeal for a change in the conduct of political affairs was the outcome of the disgust he was capable of feeling at himself and the realities of his situation. Certainly Alexander, at the time under the influence of the religious fanatic Baroness Kruedener, was prepared to believe himself the saviour of Europe and relished the prospect of a grand gesture. Most statesmen seemed embarrassed by the Tsar's enthusiasm and would have concurred in Metternich's description of the Holy Alliance as having 'no more sense or value than that of a philanthropic aspiration disguised beneath the cloak of religion'. Whatever nineteenth-century liberals alleged, the Alliance was not regarded by the Tsar as an alliance of monarchs against their subjects.

Another source of conflict in the late eighteenth century was the rivalry between Austria and Prussia in Germany. After Frederick the Great had seized Silesia from Austria in 1740 this antagonism had never been far from open war: the two states, Austria the traditionally dominant and Prussia the parvenu, had watched one another's moves, each nervous of any change that might assist the other in gaining German hegemony. The wholesale changes in Germany brought about by the Napoleonic Wars—the disappearance of the majority of small states and the dissolution of the Holy Roman Empire—had created a new situation of flux. When Russia had defeated Napoleon, and her armies were driving him back across Europe, Austria and Prussia, besides trying to forestall one another's schemes, were faced with the possibility of Russian interference.

Austria had more to fear than any other power from the prospect of an overwhelming Russian victory. At his most pessimistic the Austrian Chancellor, Metternich, imagined the sort of Russian domination in central and eastern Europe that was to occur in 1945, and with France crushed there would be no power in the west to counterbalance Russia in the way the United States was to do in 1945. Equally, Metternich feared that Russia and France might together dominate Europe, crushing the states that lay between them and dismembering the Austrian Empire. Hence Austria's aim was to contain the power of France, but not at the expense of raising up Russia.

One way in which Metternich sought to restrain Russia—and in fact Prussia as well—was by exploiting the fear of revolution and exaggerating its danger. He was able to win the rulers of these countries to policies of immobility in international affairs, ostensibly on the grounds that anything else might advance the cause of revolution in Europe, but in fact because any creative or expansionist policy which Prussia might embark on was dreaded by Austria as dangerous to herself. Collective intervention against revolution, or at least intervention that was collectively authorised,

DENMARK

SCHLESWIG-
HOLSTEIN

HANOVER   Berlin   RUSSIA

NETHERLANDS   PR USSIA   Warsaw

LUXEMBURG   Frankfurt   KINGDOM
                                 OF POLAND

                 BAVARIA

FRANCE   AUS TRIA

SWITZERLAND   Vienna   HUNGARY

SAVOY PIEDMONT

NICE   Venice

                                 TURKISH
CORSICA   PAPAL   EMPIRE
                 STATES
                 Rome

SARDINIA   Naples

                 KINGDOM OF
                 THE
                 TWO SICILIES

MALTA (British)

•••••••• FRONTIER OF GERMAN CONFEDERATION

———— FRONTIER OF AUSTRIAN EMPIRE

– – – – FRONTIER OF PRUSSIA

════ FRONTIER OF ITALY AFTER 1861

CENTRAL EUROPE 1815.

was a further way of restraining Prussia and Russia from pursuing independent policies, and at the same time associating them with Austrian actions. The Eastern Courts, linked in the popular view as the Holy Alliance, partly from panic at revolution but primarily from Metternich's desire to preserve equilibrium in Europe, came to act as a combined force against constitutional advance and political change.

A misunderstanding of the Holy Alliance, failure to judge the Tsar's intentions, belief in Talleyrand's talk of legitimacy, above all the vantage point of hindsight have led to frequent attacks on the Vienna settlement as something essentially reactionary and backward-looking. It is seen as having deliberately ignored the forces of nationalism and democracy. This charge will not really stand examination. To have created a united Germany or a uñited Italy in 1815 would have entailed using force to compel people to accept such solutions; and at least the Treaties of Vienna left the multiplicity of states in Germany and Italy greatly reduced. At the same time, the accusation of blind reaction in disregarding the wishes of peoples will not stand in view of the equally great disregard shown by the French Revolutionary government and Napoleon, supposedly champions of progress. If the test of peace is that it should leave few unexploded bombs to go off in the face of posterity, the peace of 1815, and Castlereagh's share in it, certainly deserve praise. From the point of view of Britain alone, by securing her most important gains overseas she had, in the Vienna settlement, enormously strengthened her position in the world and established the basis for her nineteenth-century ascendancy.

2 **The changing pattern**   Clearly the pattern of international relations of 1815 changed with time. First, the memories of the revolutionary and Napoleonic cataclysm grew dimmer. It became harder for Metternich to convince the rulers of Russia and Prussia that disaster lay ahead if they should pursue independent policies. The statesman and the rulers themselves changed. Alexander was replaced by his brother Nicholas, more Russian and less idiosyncratic in his policies. Castlereagh was followed by

other Foreign Secretaries, representing different governments and a changing electorate. Frederick William III of Prussia was succeeded by Frederick William IV, and revolution in France in 1830 produced a somewhat more liberal constitution and a new king. As memories of Napoleon became less haunting so traditions of co-operation, always frail, were lost and national self-interest became more powerful.

The smaller powers of Europe underwent change and new states emerged, such as Belgium and Greece. The strengths of the major powers also altered in relation to one another. Britain became increasingly powerful and rich as her industrialisation advanced. Later, Prussia was to find her scattered provinces and far-flung coalfields brought together by railways and a customs union to give her economic hegemony in Germany. France, on the other hand, was to fall behind, and her population increased more slowly than those of her rivals. She gained nothing in 1815, unlike the other major powers, and in losing the Netherlands at the Peace of Paris she lost the Belgian coalfields, whose exploitation had played a big part in her recent industrial development.

Despite these changes and whatever their different interests, a consciousness of mutual advantage still tended to hold the powers together. Thus the change of dynasty in France, the Belgian separation from Holland, the Greek revolt and rebellion in Italy and Poland did not lead to European war. Palmerston claimed in a letter to his Prime Minister in 1836 that 'the three and the two think differently and therefore act differently', contrasting Britain and France, as the constitutional powers, with the three autocratic states. Nevertheless, differences did not inhibit Palmerston from subsequently working with Russia to frustrate French policy in the Near East.

It was not until the revolutions of 1848, which occurred all over Europe, that the position was dramatically to change; but not, as European statesmen had previously feared, because revolution and a republic in France meant an immediate military descent upon her neighbours. But Metternich now at last was gone, nationalism asserted itself with a new intensity, and popular hatreds were stirred up between peoples. Even more important

Napoleon's nephew, Louis Napoleon, was brought to power in France, first as President, later as Emperor. Here at last was the ruler of one of the major European powers who, far from sharing a common interest in preservation of the status quo of 1815, could only see it as a disgrace.

It was now that the character of the period changed. In contrast to over thirty years of comparative peace, the next twenty years saw four major wars—the Crimean War of Britain and France against Russia, the Franco-Austrian War in Italy, the Austro-Prussian War and the Franco-Prussian War. Two new states emerged with the unification of Italy and Germany and the European equilibrium was dramatically upset. If equilibrium was to be restored it would have to be through a new relationship of forces, for by 1871 British statesmen were dealing with a Europe totally changed from that which had emerged from the Napoleonic Wars in 1815.

Chapter II

British interests

1 National interests—principles and pressures   Metternich believed that states had permanent interests or concerns that could be discovered and should, once revealed, be the starting point of their relations with other states. He did not accept that these interests might be subjective value judgements or even that they might be open to significant differences in interpretation. In fact, some of his dislike for Canning's conduct of Near Eastern affairs was due to resentment at what he felt to be the British Foreign Secretary's wilful disregard for fundamental British interests.

Before going on to discover whether there were such recognisable interests underlying British foreign policy from 1815 to 1865, it is important to be aware of some of the implications of the concept of national interests. First, if there is to be a common judgement of a state's interests there must be broad agreement as to what is the nature and purpose of the state. For instance, if a state is believed to be based upon the dynastic ownership of land, then clearly the interests involved are different from those of a state which is seen as the expression or formal embodiment of a sovereign people. Both these views of the nature of the state were held in Europe after 1815; for instance, the Habsburg state was founded on the Habsburg dynasty, whereas after the Revolution, especially after 1830, the French state was claimed to be the expression of the French people.

A second difficulty in identifying national interest arises from the conviction that the concerns of a single nation cannot be independent of those of mankind as a whole. Mazzini, although one of the most important publicists of the nation state, nevertheless believed that individual human progress was not really possible unless all men progressed; thus the nation would always have to take account of what was advantageous to mankind in determining what was to its own advantage. A specific case of this merging of the particular in the general interest was the belief held by many people in nineteenth-century Britain that competition and free trade throughout the world were required for significant growth in Britain's wealth.

The nature of the British constitution made agreement on national interest unlikely in the nineteenth century. In the shaping and direction of his policy a British Foreign Secretary could not merely follow his own judgement. The Sovereign, the permanent staff of his department, the Cabinet of which he was a member, Parliament, the electorate, and even the voteless majority of the people had all to be considered and would very often have different ideas as to what was in Britain's interest. Castlereagh recognised this in his State Paper of 1820: 'The King of Great Britain, from the nature of our constitution, has . . . all his means to acquire through Parliament, and he must well know that if embarked in a War, which the Voice of the Country does not support, the Efforts of the strongest Administration which ever served the Crown would soon be unequal to the prosecution of the Contest.' Certainly there was little chance of British interest being confused with dynastic interest by 1815; nevertheless the monarchy sometimes had different views from the Government as to what was important. Personal likes and dislikes—George IV's pique with Tsar Alexander, and Queen Victoria's liking for Napoleon III—could influence judgement of policy, but the most obvious source of disagreement between King and Ministers at the beginning of the period was Hanover. As rulers of Hanover, George III and his sons had interests apart from those of Britain.

Castlereagh was influential enough to be able to treat Hanoverian foreign policy as the province of the British Government as well as that of his King, but when Canning was Foreign Secretary, George IV refused to accept this position and carried on a secret diplomacy through Count Munster, his Hanoverian minister in London. William IV took less interest in Hanoverian affairs, and the two states were seperated in 1837 when Victoria succeeded to the English throne and her uncle, by Salic Law, ruled in Hanover. The accession of a young, inexperienced girl did not mean, however, the end of conflict between Crown and Ministers in foreign policy. The influence of her uncle, King Leopold of Belgium, and most of all, of her husband Prince Albert, her stubbornness, her increasing family ties with other rulers and later, her long familiarity with affairs of the state, meant that Victoria's views often differed from those of her ministers.

In no sense, however, was there a royal foreign policy as distinct from that of the Government, as sometimes happened in France, notably under Louis Napoleon. Also in contrast to France, the Foreign Office cannot be seen in the period as having a policy of its own which it was able to foist upon ministers. The smallness of the staff left much of the work to the Foreign Secretary himself, but in any case the strength of character of such men as Castlereagh, Canning and Palmerston would have prevented any development of an independent Foreign Office policy. It is true that because of their remoteness, particularly before telegraph lines were laid, ambassadors did from time to time have great powers of initiative, but it was very rare for them to pursue policies which were based upon an individual interpretation of British interests.

Where the real room for disagreement lay was in the relationship of a Foreign Secretary to his colleagues in the Cabinet, to Parliament and to the people. Canning, Castlereagh and Palmerston were all remarkably determined men and were not dominated by their Prime Ministers, but Palmerston continued to be very influential in the formulation of foreign policy when he was himself Prime Minister. The usual reason for disagreement was that the Foreign Secretary, preoccupied by external events, found that his colleagues were prompted on the other hand by domestic factors to consider British interests best served by inaction.

At some times in British history, foreign policy has been much influenced by party differences. Between 1815 and 1865, however, parties were not so strong, nor so mutually exclusive, as to give clear guidelines to national interest. Nevertheless Whig and Liberal governments were more favourable to constitutional and nationalist advance in Europe than were Tory Cabinets. There was, for instance, a clear distinction between the conservative views of the Duke of Wellington and the progressive attitudes of Lord John Russell, but Canning, a Tory, favoured the progressive cause in Europe much more than most Whigs. Rather than look for differences based upon party it is more helpful to contrast the typical government attitude to British interests, which tended to be empirical and practical, with popular views, which were often ideological and romantic. The latter could be nationalistic—what was later in the century to be called jingoistic, or progressive and anti-reactionary.

Finally, from the back benches of both government and opposition there was a disinclination to accept that British interests might necessitate the spending of large sums of money. Melbourne advised Palmerston to 'recollect that powerful ministries have in general found themselves unable to incline this nation to vindicate her rights in distant countries', and fear of the cost was the most important reason for this. 'Public opinion influenced foreign policies in various ways, but most persistently through parliamentary control of the purse', writes C. J. Bartlett.

2 A nation of shopkeepers James Joll in his introduction to *Britain and Europe* writes: 'British interests are those arising out of Britain's position as a maritime and commercial power.' At its simplest, this means that since all trade and commerce came and went by sea, any British government should seek to command, or prevent any rival from commanding, the sea lanes. This had been realised long before 1815 and was to remain a cardinal point of British policy throughout the period. At the outset, in the peace treaties which followed Napoleon's defeat, British intentions can be discerned in the return of the East Indies to Holland— probably the richest of European colonies—and the retention of the Cape of Good Hope, Malta and Heligoland, all of which seemed to have commanding strategic positions. Again, Britain claimed her right to visit and search other vessels at sea until 1858, something which in time of war seemed necessary to protect her maritime position. Above all, Britain sought to maintain her naval supremacy by having not only the largest navy in the world but one that was larger than the combined navies of any other two states—what was later to be known as the 'Two-Power Standard'.

The Earl of Granville, when he was Foreign Secretary, issued a general statement of policy in which he averred that 'one of the first duties of a British Government must always be to obtain for our Foreign Trade that security which is essential to its success'. There was, however, much more to this security than merely holding key strategic points and maintaining a great navy. As Britain was a trading nation her subjects travelled and resided all over the world and the British government had to take steps to ensure their security. If they were at sea in merchant vessels the government must seek to protect them from piracy, and when conflicts broke out which led to fighting at sea, British Foreign Secretaries acted to minimise the danger to the mercantile marine.

It was not only on the high seas, however, that British subjects required security. Because there were Britons living in so many countries it was particularly important that Britain should be diplomatically represented throughout the world. The government was always aware of the need to represent its subjects, wherever they might be, despite the Earl of Clarendon's impatience, when Foreign Secretary, at what he described as demands for help from Englishmen whenever they received a black eye. Sometimes action taken by the government might seem totally disproportionate to the offence, but it was usually founded on a belief, however misguided, that unless action was strong British merchants would suffer further injustice. Palmerston epitomised this view at its most outrageous when he asserted: 'These half-civilised governments . . . all require a dressing every eight or ten years to keep them in order, their minds are too shallow to receive an impression that will last longer than some such period and warning is of little use.' Very often, however, the economic interests of foreign states could be relied upon to secure fair treatment for British traders abroad. Bartlett affirms that 'it was only when local factionalism in, for instance, Buenos Aires was no longer restrained by economic rationalisation that gunboats became essential'.

The incident which caused the most anger in Parliament as well as abroad was concerned with demands for succour from a Portuguese resident in Athens, Don Pacifico, who claimed British citizenship because he had been born in Gibraltar. His house was gutted in a riot in 1847 and he unsuccessfully claimed over £80,000 damages. The Greek government were so slow in making any offer that Palmerston in 1850 ordered the Mediterranean fleet to the Piraeus, there to seize Greek shipping as surety. After this the Greek government speedily agreed to pay Don Pacifico his compensation. Another incident in which Britain seemed to over-react followed the arrest by the Chinese of men believed to be notorious pirates from a ship, the *Arrow*, which was flying the British flag, the owner being a Chinese resident of Hong Kong. Again British rights were being invoked for somewhat disreputable reasons.

Both the Don Pacifico and the *Arrow* incidents followed a period of difficulty with the governments concerned. The problem of the Far East was particularly intractable because of the clash of fundamentally different cultures and attitudes. It is perhaps arguable that no country has the right to isolate itself from the rest of the world. Certainly the *Edinburgh Review* argued that none had: 'The Japanese undoubtedly have an exclusive right to the possession of their territory; but they must not abuse that right to the extent of debarring all other nations from a participation in its riches and virtues.' Lest this too easily be assumed to be pure cant masking the avarice of selfish traders, it should be remembered that many people in Britain in the middle of the nineteenth century believed Free Trade was necessary for human progress. Recession in Europe merely strengthened the determination of British and other European business men to increase greatly their trade with the Far East. That this sentiment was shared by politicians is shown by Palmerston's statement that 'the rivalship of European manufacturers is fast excluding our productions from the markets of Europe, and we must unremittingly endeavour to find in other parts of the world new vents for the produce of our industry'.

The clash between traders who were anxious to penetrate further and countries that wished to restrict and even exclude them would anyhow have made for difficulty. What exacerbated the situation in China was that the Government of India Act of 1833 opened the Chinese trade to all British subjects, ending the monopoly of the East India Company. This change increased the number of merchants trying to trade with China but, more important, it meant that no longer would the Company superintend intercourse between the Chinese and the British. The British government intended to open normal diplomatic relations, but at once found that the Chinese were not prepared to consent. They refused to accept the credentials of foreign representatives as conveying any special status, and the first, Lord Napier, was publicly stigmatised as a 'lawless foreign slave' and a 'dog barbarian'. The Chinese believed that anyone in their territories acquired the position of a subject of the Emperor and was therefore totally accountable to him. In this conflict of principle a compromise was unlikely, and wars duly followed. British technical superiority led to success, and in 1842 the Treaty of Nankin ceded Hong Kong as a base to Britain and opened an additional five Chinese ports to foreign traders. A further round of fighting occurred in 1857–8, however, before the Treaty of Tientsin established something like full diplomatic relations between China and Britain, marking, *The Cambridge History of British Foreign Policy* claims, the end 'of a struggle of two-and-a-half centuries waged by Western nations to obtain for their Ambassadors what they considered to be their proper position at an Eastern Court'.

The Chinese Wars, however, seem to involve something other than the mere protection of British subjects; they appear as part of a government policy of actively supporting the extension of British trade. This is particularly true of the First Chinese War—the Opium War—where the actual outbreak of hostilities occurred over a Chinese attempt to confiscate British-owned supplies of opium in an endeavour to end the opium trade, legally banned but hitherto connived at, between China and India.

In a mercantilist age there would have been nothing strange in forceful government action to extend British trade. Although some of the apparatus of mercantilism such as the Navigation Laws was not finally relinquished until the middle of the nineteenth century, it was in the main a discredited policy, and governments were rather concerned to work towards cutting tariffs and prohibitions on trade. Palmerston used the occasion of the revision of a commercial treaty with Portugal to express his attitude: 'My doctrine is that exclusive commercial privileges are of no real advantage to a country. All we want is free trade and open competition.' An example of government action of this sort is the Commercial Treaty with France of 1860, which was negotiated by Cobden with the backing of Gladstone as Chancellor of the Exchequer. This treaty, described by one historian as 'certainly one of the landmarks in the fiscal history of Europe in the nineteenth century', by cutting tariffs allowed French imports of British manufactured goods and British imports of French wine to be more than doubled in the first decade after it had been signed. In its negotiations with the Zollverein (the Prussian-led customs league which was to spread through Germany) the British government first sought to check the growth of the league, and only when that failed, to concentrate upon securing beneficial terms for British trade.

Some writers have attempted to show that the desire to extend trade played a decisive role in the formulation of British foreign policy. Thus, increasing trade with the Levant and impatience with the monopolistic policies of Mehemet Ali, Pasha of Egypt, have been claimed to lie behind British Near Eastern policy. Metternich's biographer Srbik has argued that Palmerston's desire to create an independent Belgium after 1830 was the result of hopes that this would fatally weaken Holland's industry, which might increasingly have rivalled that of Britain. Even if this is far-fetched it is probably true that it was economic rivalry between Britain and France which prevented their *entente* of the 1830s from becoming something more permanent. Palmerston complained in 1837 that the French were driven by 'jealousy of the commercial prosperity of England and a desire to arrest the progress of that prosperity'. Britain was, however, fortunate in that until the last quarter of the nineteenth century she was so advanced industrially that she need ask only for competition on equal terms to be sure of success.

3 British interests in the New World   Britain had considerable economic and political interests in the New World, interests which had become stronger through the development of trade with Latin America during the Napoleonic Wars and were to be further strengthened with the investment of British capital in the industrialisation of the United States. As well as this direct concern Britain also had a crucial rôle to play in American relationships with Europe because her naval ascendancy gave her virtual control of the Atlantic.

This naval predominance, for example, rendered decisive Britain's part in the attempts of the Latin American empires of Spain and Portugal to break away from their parent states at the outset of the period. These revolts faced Britain with a clash between the urgings of her European allies that monarchical rule should be restored and her own economic interests, which dictated friendly relations with the emergent states. Even after the South American empires had won their independence the problem persisted in the Caribbean with, for instance, Spanish attempts to hold Cuba, and in Central America, where as late as the 1860s Louis Napoleon involved himself in the troubled affairs of Mexico.

More intractable were Britain's relations with the United States; the two powers besides being important trading partners were rivals throughout the New World. Canning voiced British suspicion in 1826: 'The avowed pretension of the United States to put themselves at the head of a confederacy against Europe (Great Britain included) is *not* a pretension identified with our interests, or one that we can countenance as tolerable.' The 'pretension' adopted by Presidents Monroe and Polk was one that many Americans supported and was to be the basis of American policy for much of the century.

Underlying all points of difference between the United States and Britain was the mutual distrust and bitterness engendered by the past. The United States, having recently won its independence, drifted into war again with Britain in 1812, and the Treaty of Ghent in 1814 did not heal the divisions. The Americans distrusted all British motives in the New World and lost no opportunity to rejoice in any discomfiture for Britain. Professor Newton has written of a legend 'ineradicably planted in the public mind' which had a permanent influence on the American outlook on foreign events, and 'implied in every glorification of the greatness of the United States and every incitement to patriotism a belittlement of British efforts and aversion to Great Britain as the only enemy'. However understandable such a view might be in a newly independent state, it had a pernicious influence upon relations between the two countries and demanded a statesmanlike imperviousness from British diplomats to prevent a succession of crises.

In South America there was little chance of the United States achieving hegemony. In the Caribbean and Central America, however, it was a different story. Here, United States influence was much greater, and disputes over Cuba, Nicaragua and Honduras threatened relations between the two powers to the point of war. Sensitivity over the future of Central America was heightened because by the 1840s there were projects under discussion for the construction of a canal between the Pacific and the Atlantic, and control of the surrounding land would be of critical importance. Concern over Central America and Cuba was in the main the preoccupation of Americans from the Southern States, the Northerners being more worried about relations with Canada. Fishing rights and access to one another's markets—

especially when British moves to free trade had the effect of ending Canada's favoured treatment in the British West Indies—both proved to be subjects for argument. The really explosive issue, however, was the frontier between the two countries. At its most extreme this grew into attempts by citizens of the United States at outright annexation, as when insurgents in Upper Canada in 1837 received help and supplies from the State of New York, and when disputes over the Oregon territory in the mid-1840s necessitated British military reinforcement of Canada.

Another sensitive issue was Britain's claim to maritime rights, in particular, to visit and search neutral merchant ships. The assertion of this claim, leading to the subsequent impressment into the Royal Navy of sailors claimed to be British subjects but regarded by the United States as their naturalised citizens had been one of the causes of war in 1812. Long after the war was over America refused to countenance the principle urged by Britain that their navies should be allowed mutual rights to visit and search ships which they suspected of carrying slaves. It is true that other countries disliked the scheme, since the relative size of fleets meant that the right would most usually be exercised by Britain, but the United States was particularly intransigent. In the words of President Taylor in 1841, 'However desirous the United States may be for the suppression of the Slave-trade, they cannot consent to interpolations into the maritime code at the mere will and pleasure of other governments.' This lack of co-operation considerably antagonised feeling in Britain, which was dedicated to the ending of the traffic. American inflexibility partly resulted from the deliberate policy of those who supported slavery, and thus it was not until the Civil War and the ending of slavery that the matter was finally laid to rest. By that time Britain had modified her maritime claims.

In 1861 the American Civil War broke out and Britain's relations with America became most difficult. British interests were not obvious, particularly with the swaying fortunes of the two sides. On the one hand the secessionist Southern Confederacy pleaded for recognition, on the other hand the Federal government was eager to construe any British act as unfriendly and a breach of neutrality. The position was considerably complicated by the importance of the Southern States as the source of some four-fifths of the raw material for Lancashire's cotton industry, upon which, it has been estimated, over 500,000 people directly depended for their livelihood. These supplies were cut off by the Federal government's blockade of the South, a situation which provided a standing invitation to attempt blockade-breaking.

At one point Southern military success seemed to portend the failure of the North to enforce the Union. W. E. Gladstone, then Chancellor of the Exchequer, declared, 'Jefferson Davis and other leaders of the South have made a nation. We may anticipate with certainty the success of the Southern States so far as their separation from the North is concerned.' However, commercial and industrial opinion was shocked by fears that this might imply Britain's entry into the war. Lord Derby, the Conservative leader, asserted that recognition of the South could be of no value unless Britain was prepared to engage in hostilities against the North; nothing was done before the tide of war turned and the North emerged as the likely victor. Relations, however, remained difficult.

The Federal government bitterly resented the inaction of the British government in allowing the construction of ships in British yards which, it was alleged, were to be delivered to the Southern States to prey upon Northern shipping. One such vessel, the *Alabama*, was allowed to leave Britain despite repeated warnings, and proceeded to wreak devastation upon the commerce of the Northern States and to remain a source of disagreement between the two countries long after the Civil War was over.

4 British interests and the balance of power Although Britain's interests in Europe were partly the result of her needs as a commercial power they covered a wider field. Contiguous states tend to enmity, and consequently search for allies amongst one another's neighbours—what Sir Lewis Namier described as the 'sandwich system of international politics'. Nineteenth-century Britain, however, was in a somewhat more complicated position than a mere layer in a European sandwich; her frontier was the sea, and hence all maritime powers were her neighbours. Of course, France as the nearest was most to be feared, but more distant ones could never be ignored. As a corollary, however, there existed a wide choice of possible allies.

A threat to British security from the Continent might take two forms; one direct, one more indirect. First there was the possibility of military invasion, and even after 1815 there were scares of this nature although British naval pre-eminence had never been more marked. Secondly there was the possibility of blockade and embargo being used in an endeavour to starve Britain into surrender, with harassment of her sea-routes and continental ports closed to her ships. In both cases a hostile state would need to be certain of European support; otherwise her armies would be distracted by being engaged at home and the blockade would not be effective. A continental alliance against Britain would always be difficult to construct and would be unlikely to last. Thus Britain's principal cause for fear was that one state might achieve a European hegemony, and to prevent this was her fundamental interest.

One region which has frequently been the battleground of struggles for European predominance is the Low Countries. To Britain this was a particularly sensitive area; its geographical proximity and its maritime position as the location of vital ports had made its neutrality a critical British interest. It was French expansion into the area that Britain most feared, and it was from France that she expected any attempts at European predominance. Britain also wished to preserve the neutrality of the Iberian peninsula, particularly Portugal. In times past Spain had posed a direct naval threat, but the importance of the peninsula lay in its strategic position, commanding the Atlantic and Mediterranean routes; again it was French involvement that was most feared.

Another sensitive area was the Near East—roughly the southeastern borderland of Europe. The threat here was thought to be Russian rather than French. It was believed that the Russians aimed at the defeat and conquest of the Ottoman Empire and the possession of Constantinople. Disraeli expressed Britain's fears very clearly: 'If the Russians had Constantinople, they could at any time march their way through Syria to the mouth of the Nile . . . Constantinople is the key of India.' The Ottoman Empire should thus be maintained and, with one brief exception, British governments throughout the period believed this to be a firm interest.

It was not just in the Near East that Russia was feared, but all along her southern border. In 1840 Palmerston voiced a fear that was fairly general in Britain: 'It seems pretty clear that sooner or later the Cossak and the Sepoy, the man from the Baltic and from the British islands will meet in the centre of Asia.' Between 1839 and 1842 Britain and Russia collided, as Russia infiltrated Persia and Britain sought to intervene in Afghanistan. Later, in the 1860s, the Russians seized several Asiatic regions such as Turkestan and Bokhara. It was thought that Russia might march on India or else sever the routes to India through Western and Central Asia. In both cases she would be able to exert military pressure without the possibility of intervention by the Royal Navy. No other European power could offer a similar threat. It may be that, as the Marquis of Salisbury was later to claim, this fear of Russia was chimerical and the result of British statesmen using maps on too small a scale; certainly the distances were immense. Nevertheless, particularly before the construction of the Suez Canal and the consequent decline of the overland route via Syria and the Persian Gulf, the Russian threat to British communications with India was genuinely felt.

Because of this apprehension it was reckoned by successive British governments to be in Britain's interest to preserve the states whose collapse would favour Russian power. The Ottoman Empire, of course, came into this category, as did Austria—at least as a Central European Power, though there was some doubt over her Italian position. In the Baltic Palmerston considered that Denmark should be encouraged, and this was the basis of his dislike of an anti-Danish solution to the problem of Schleswig-Holstein.

The phrase which recurs in describing British endeavours to maintain her security is *balance of power*. From the outset it is important to realise that the phrase has been employed in contradictory ways. Martin Wight, in an essay in *Diplomatic Investigations*, carries conviction when he argues that the phrase has nine separate meanings. It can vary from a belief in the existence of 'an inherent tendency of international politics to produce an even distribution of power' to support of 'the existing distribution of power'. A further complication is that sometimes the term is employed to describe a situation where one nation possesses a 'special role in maintaining an even distribution of power'. This use appears in Palmerston's avowal to William IV in 1832 'that by throwing the moral influence of Great Britain into one scale or the other ... Your Majesty may ... become on many occasions the arbiter of events in Europe'.

Whether exponents of the balance of power as the basic British interest in European policy saw Britain as an integral part of the system or as normally outside it, intervening only to redress imbalance, it was generally held to militate against the predominance of any European Power. This was the belief of Lord John Russell when he affirmed: 'The balance of power in Europe means in effect the independence of its several states. The preponderance of any one Power threatens and destroys this independence.' After 1815 Britain was tolerably well pleased with the status quo on the Continent and therefore invoked the concept of balance or equilibrium to preserve it. Outside Europe, however, a very different situation pertained. Here Britain had predominance and strove to maintain it. Again, however, this could be justified in British eyes by the notion of balance of power. Perhaps the best example is from the eighteenth century, when George III wrote to Catherine of Russia inviting her help to restore the balance of power in the sense of restoring Britain's supremacy at sea. It is not surprising that this was a much more popular principle with British than with continental statesmen.

Opponents of the concept as a major interest in foreign policy have likewise differed as to its precise meaning. It has been portrayed as something secretive and disreputable, a process leading to such situations as the partition of Poland. It is in this sense that President Wilson rejoiced before Congress in 1918 in the death of 'the great game, now forever discredited, of the balance of power'. The most vigorous attacks on the concept in Britain during the nineteenth century came from Cobden and Bright. Bright, speaking in the House of Commons, argued: 'This whole notion of the "balance of power" is a mischievous delusion which has come down to us from past times.' Cobden believed 'the theory of a balance of power is a mere chimera', and both he and Bright pointed to the failure of the concept to take account of changes in relative power following upon population increase or industrial growth. 'Might not Austria complain', asked Bright, 'that we have disturbed the "balance of power" because we are growing so much stronger . . . from wealth that is created by the hard labours and skill of our population?'

What Cobden and Bright attacked most bitterly was what they saw as Britain's gratuitous interference in unnecessary matters, often undertaken in the name of upholding the balance of power. They believed that Britain's interests would be best served by a cheap foreign policy based upon cutting down armaments and relying upon Free Trade—in James Joll's words, 'not merely as an economic doctrine but also as a basis for international political organisation'.

In the period after 1815 there were few in Britain who really believed that she could isolate herself from the Continent. Nevertheless there was a very real difference in Parliament and among Foreign Secretaries as to the extent of Britain's involvement. One view was that Britain should only be concerned with a few special interests; according to the other she was part of Europe and all that happened there had significance for her. Palmerston expressed the latter view very forcibly when he stated: 'Whatever affects the general condition of Europe or of any important part of it, is a legitimate object of solicitude to England.' Sometimes the controversy is described as being between *intervention* and *non-intervention*, at other times as *internationalism* against *isolationism*. The former particularly is misleading because it tends to group together intervention for purposes of maintaining the status quo with intervention to upset it. For instance, it is difficult to see very much help in a classification which includes those Radicals who attacked Palmerston for not helping Hungary in 1849, Palmerston himself for his endeavours on the side of the Spanish Liberals, and Castlereagh for his alleged involvement of Britain in the reactionary policies of the continental Powers. Perhaps Donald Southgate is correct when he argues in *The Passing of the Whigs* that differences of policy 'appear on analysis to lie less in ideology or party than temperament'. He maintains that 'the true line of division is not between Whig and Tory, but between activists like Canning, Palmerston, Russell . . . and passivists like Aberdeen, Malmesbury, Granville'.

In his famous State Paper of 1820 Castlereagh declared: 'We shall be found in our place when actual danger menaces the system of Europe, but the Country cannot, and will not act upon abstract and speculative Principles of Precaution.' This did not mean, however, that Castlereagh believed Britain should wait for crises to develop on the Continent before taking action, merely that she reserved the right to act as she wished rather than on predetermined lines. Castlereagh saw the need for Britain to intervene to prevent situations from developing which might prove dangerous; his immediate response to the outbreak of the Greek revolt against the Turks is a clear example of this. Despite differences in character between them, Castlereagh, Canning and Palmerston were men who could not accept a quietist role of waiting on events. The Marquis of Salisbury was to assert, later in the century, 'English policy is to float lazily downstream, occasionally putting out a diplomatic boat-hook to avoid collisions.' Such a description would never be adequate for the policies of Castlereagh, Canning and Palmerston. They might differ in the handling of their boat-hooks and in their choice of hazards to fend off, but they were alike in the energy they expended in their watch for perils ahead and their skill in finding the strongest current. Castlereagh advocated an active policy despite the unpopularity it brought him, because he believed it to be in Britain's interest. Canning likewise believed that an active policy was in Britain's interest, but calculated that, carefully presented, it would bring him popularity and political strength. Palmerston was an activist because he felt it essential to Britain's interest, and he too calculated that it could bring him popularity and political strength. Moreover, he seemed to consider it only proper that Britain should try to shape events in Europe. In a speech to Parliament in 1849 Palmerston contended that 'it is not fitting that a country occupying such a proud position as England—that a country having such various and extensive interests, should lock herself up in a simple regard to her own internal affairs, and should be a passive and mute spectator of everything that is going on around'.

Opinions varied as to the advantage Britain gained from supporting the creation of constitutional regimes on the Continent. Palmerston had no doubt: 'In Spain, as in Portugal, the question was between arbitrary rule and constitutional and parliamentary government, and in relation to Spain, as well as to Portugal, we thought that the interests of England in every point of view, commercial and political, would be benefited by the establishment of constitutional government.' Sir Robert Peel doubted if British action served any purpose. 'It is', he told Parliament, 'my firm belief that you will not advance the cause of constitutional government by attempting to dictate to other nations . . . If you succeed, I doubt whether the institutions that take root under your patronage will be lasting. Constitutional liberty will be best worked out by those who aspire to freedom by their own efforts.'

Palmerston also incurred attack by his policy of giving advice and encouragement which he did not intend and was unable physically to reinforce; the Poles and the Danes were both perhaps misled in his last years in this way. The result was seen as a humiliation to Britain and certainly not in her interests. Writing in 1864 the future Marquis of Salisbury affirmed: 'Her [Britain's] influence in the councils of Europe has passed away . . . Our courage is not only disbelieved, but it is ridiculed as an imposture that has been found out.' Castlereagh had long before, in 1820, warned that 'unless we are prepared to support our interference with force, our judgement or advice is likely to be but rarely listened to, and would by frequent repetition soon fall into complete contempt'. Palmerston argued on the contrary, 'Opinions, if they are founded in truth and justice, will in the end prevail against the bayonets of infantry, the fire of artillery, and the charges of cavalry.'

It was not coincidence that Palmerston's European policy was declining in success and popularity by the end of his life. The British people had been somewhat disenchanted by the experience of the Crimean War as an essay in European involvement. This was not the reason, however, for the decline in Palmerston's effectiveness, nor was it that Cobden and Bright had been successful in urging a low-key foreign policy; rather it was that the European situation itself was changing. There had been a great diplomatic transformation since the Crimean War. The Revolutionary and Napoleonic Wars had left a legacy of distrust and fear of France in the rulers of Austria, Prussia and Russia which, reinforced by the July revolution of 1830, helped to hold these three states together. This had made it possible for Britain to tilt the balance between them and France, secure in the knowledge that France would be resisted by the Eastern Powers if necessary. It was this that helped Palmerston in one of his greatest triumphs, when he secured Belgian independence by using France against the Eastern Powers and then the Eastern Powers against France. By 1860 this was no longer possible, for the solidarity of the Eastern Powers was gone. At the same time the 1860s, with the creation of new states and great technical advances, were a decade of change in Europe which, writes Southgate, 'required of Britain either a costly involvement which, when it came to the crunch, her people would not face or a dignified withdrawal for which, in time, the people and the politicians opted.' The next period would see, in Seton-Watson's words, a 'deliberate abstention from continental affairs'. Symbolic of this change in Britain's appreciation of her interests was an alteration in the wording of the Mutiny Bill of 1868; no longer was it attested that the British Army was essential for the preservation of the balance of power in Europe.

Chapter III

Castlereagh

1 The man and his reputation The American historian Henry Kissinger has written: 'Castlereagh walked his solitary path, as humanly unapproachable as his policy came to be incomprehensible to the majority of his countrymen.' This might suggest that, to the writer, Castlereagh is not a very promising subject. However, with time and the perspective that it brings, his policies are not so incomprehensible, and although he was distant and unapproachable to many of those he encountered, Castlereagh's personality and character emerge as distinctive and powerful.

Perhaps the most obvious qualities of Lord Castlereagh were his tenacity of purpose and his prodigious industry. The diarist Greville wrote of Castlereagh's determination, 'which gave an appearance of resolution and confidence to all his actions, inspired his friends with admiration and excessive devotion to him and caused him to be respected by his most violent opponents'. He would continue to work towards the end he desired when to others it seemed that he could not succeed. This was shown early in his public career in his confidence that the Irish parliament could be induced to vote for union with England after having once defeated the proposal. 'I am persuaded firmness

will carry the measure', he wrote. The same quality was demonstrated at the end of his life in the way Castlereagh still fought
to preserve the European alliance which he had laboured to form.

With this perseverance went personal bravery, typified when
he was most unpopular by his disregard for the fury of the
London crowd; in one instance mingling with those attacking his
house and subsequently closing the shutters of his windows
while under a barrage of stones. This bravery could extend to
taking political chances. In the peace negotiations at Vienna,
Castlereagh broke with the instructions he had had from a
cautious Cabinet and signed a secret treaty with Austria and
France to oppose Russian and Prussian designs over Poland and
and Saxony.

In his negotiations over Saxony and Poland, Castlereagh used
reticence as a way of avoiding hostility to his policy. However,
his uncommunicativeness and obscurity were not always the
result of deliberate intent. Partly his failure to communicate
resulted from the awkward and diffuse style of both his speeches
and his writing. Canning cried, 'I'd rather fight than read it, by
God', when he received Castlereagh's three-page challenge to a
duel. Greville observed, 'As a speaker he was prolix, monotonous
and never eloquent.' Nevertheless his fine presence, his resolution and his remarkable memory made him effective in debate;
otherwise he would not have successfully led the House of
Commons for ten years. Above all, however, Castlereagh was
incomprehensible because he never grasped the importance of
explaining his policies and thus rendering them palatable to
others. He seems to have felt that the right policy would necessarily
commend itself to all but the prejudiced. Revealing in this context
is an observation he made in 1821 over his unexpected public
acclaim in a tour of Ireland: 'I am grown as popular in 1821 as
unpopular formerly, and with as little merit, and of the two unpopularity is the more convenient and gentlemanlike'. It is in-
conceivable that Canning, by contrast so successful in selling his
policies, would have ever shared such a sentiment.

If obscure, Castlereagh was rarely devious; rather he was
direct and sincere, with a laudable absence of vindictiveness, on

both a personal and a public level. The bitter quarrel with Canning which led to a duel in 1809 left surprisingly little rancour in Castlereagh, justifying the Duke of Wellington's remark on Canning's succession to Castlereagh's offices that could the latter 'look out of his grave, he would approve the appointment'.

His powers of work, his seriousness of purpose and his judgement combined to give Castlereagh stature as a politician. One Member of Parliament described him as 'a splendid summit of bright and polished frost which, like travellers in Switzerland, we all admire; but which no one can hope, and few would wish, to reach!' Indeed, many of his contemporaries saw him as aloof and impenetrable. Castlereagh might appear glacial; certainly he was shy. 'It is is strange how timid he is in society, as if he were just beginning', wrote the wife of the Russian ambassador. Nevertheless he did have charm and grace, while descriptions and portraits testify to striking handsomeness.

Robert Stewart, Viscount Castlereagh, became Second Marquis of Londonderry on his father's death in 1821. He had been born in 1769, on his father's side of Ulster-Scottish descent; his mother, like his step-mother, came from a powerful aristocratic family with considerable influence in England. Before entering the Irish Parliament in 1790, Castlereagh was educated in Ireland and then at Cambridge. His part as Chief Secretary in securing the passage of the Act of Union with England was crucial, and he was soon in office after taking his seat in the new Parliament in London in 1801. Save for the one year, he was in government—first as President of the Board of Control for India and then as Secretary of State for War and the Colonies—until 1809, when he resigned at the time of his duel with Canning. However, in 1812 he returned to office as Foreign Secretary and Leader of the House of Commons, both of which posts he was to hold until his suicide in 1822.

Despite this extensive public career at the centre of events, Castlereagh's life long awaited any serious study. It was not until 1848 that even an article was written, and that appeared in answer to the publication by his half-brother of a collection of Castlereagh's correspondence together with a short memoir. A rather lame official biography followed in 1861 which bracketed him with his half-brother, Lord Stewart, as twin subjects. Only then Robert Cecil, himself later to become a distinguished statesman as the Marquis of Salisbury, made an attempt to rescue Castlereagh's reputation from oblivion. Cecil concluded that Castlereagh's 'was that rare phenomenon—a practical man of the highest order, who yet did not forfeit his title to be considered a man of genius'. Then gradually, as his career came to be thought worthy of study, Castlereagh's reputation advanced until he is now generally accepted as one of the very greatest of British Foreign Secretaries.

The researches of Sir Charles Webster into his foreign policy displayed for the first time the full stature of the man, and subsequent studies have confirmed that historian's findings. Since Robert Cecil, professional diplomatists in particular have praised him, and it is no accident that one who wrote most glowingly of Castlereagh, Sir Harold Nicolson, was himself a diplomat at the Peace Conference which followed the First World War. For the failures of the Peace of Versailles have been instrumental in the rehabilitation of the peacemakers of Vienna. Even now, however, surprisingly few books have been written about Castlereagh.

The chief reason for this long neglect was the dominance during much of the nineteenth century of Radical and Whig writers who saw Castlereagh as totally discredited, an unsuccessful Conservative who had sought to check proper progress. The taunts of the romantic poets, the gossip of jealous contemporaries and the works of pamphleteers were taken as serious evaluations and accepted canon. Even today it is the historians of the Left, such as E. J. Hobsbawm in *The Age of Revolution* and E. P. Thompson in *The Making of the English Working Class*, who are most reluctant to praise Castlereagh.

It seems, however, that more than his conservatism is needed to explain Castlereagh's lack of reputation, since other Tories such as the Duke of Wellington who were more extreme in their views did not share his fate. No wholly satisfactory answer exists, but undoubtedly Castlereagh's inability and unwillingness to explain what he was trying to achieve must bear some of the blame.

With time, his speeches and his writings have become no easier to follow.

2 The man of reaction

> The vulgarest tool that Tyranny could want,
> With just enough of talent, and no more
> To lengthen fetters by another fix'd,
> And offer poison long already mix'd.

This view of Castlereagh which Byron offered in his dedication of *Don Juan* was one which many others shared. He was seen as being responsible as a sort of "hatchet man" for the destruction of liberties all over Europe. Creevey wrote of him as spending his 'whole life in an avowed, cold-blooded contempt of every honest public principle'. Shelley in *The Mask of Anarchy* also portrayed him as a man of blood:

> I met Murder in the way—
> He had a mask like Castlereagh.

To some extent this impression of Castlereagh as a reactionary is the product of his reputation in home affairs. As the man who was probably most concerned with securing union between England and Ireland, Castlereagh was attacked as the murderer of Ireland's liberties. Later it fell to him to be the chief government apologist in the House of Commons for the repressive policies pursued in the difficult period after the end of the Napoleonic Wars. Whether such a reputation for tyranny and the disregard for the liberties of others is deserved is uncertain; with respect to Ireland it would seem to have little basis in fact. What is certain is that such a reputation coloured men's opinions of Castlereagh's foreign policy.

Nevertheless his foreign policy in itself was attacked as reactionary. Castlereagh's part in the defeat of Napoleon and in the peace settlement which followed earned him a share in the general odium felt by many progressives in Europe for the victors of 1814–15. The extinction of republics such as Genoa and Venice, and what was felt to be neglect of constitutional and national principles, were condemned as the fruits of blind reaction.

Finally his attachment to the Alliance after 1815 and his involvement in the Congresses, as well as being attacked as anti-British,
were introduced as evidence of Castlereagh's subjection to
Metternich and therefore of his belief in the Austrian Chancellor's
policies of international intervention on the side of repression.

Something has already been said of the futility of blaming the
statesmen of Vienna for not creating nation states in Germany and
Italy; such measures in 1815 were not feasible. Whether Britain
should have done more to obtain constitutions for countries
handed back to their former rulers is a different matter. Certainly,
unless Britain's interest demanded it, Castlereagh was no more
prepared to intervene to create constitutions than he was to
intervene to crush them. However strange it may seem in one
who has been attacked for a lack of patriotism in his policies, the
question of independence or freedom was not the vital one to
Castlereagh; rather it was where lay the interest of Britain, as
expressed in order and peace. Small states such as Genoa, which
without regard to the wishes of their inhabitants were given to
larger ones in the settlement, were believed by Castlereagh to
have forfeited their title to independence by the ease with which
France had overrun them. Stability was not to be achieved in
Europe with a mass of small states that invited—and could not
repel—aggression from outside. Castlereagh certainly preferred
monarchy to republicanism, and Conservatism to liberalism, but
he was not prepared to commit Britain to policies of combating
liberalism and nationalism unless they seemed to threaten
Britain's interests directly, as his policy over Spain, the Spanish
colonies, and Naples so clearly shows.

There was one aspect of Castlereagh's foreign policy where he
worked squarely on the side of progressives—in his attempt to
secure the abandonment of the slave trade. Earlier in his career
Castlereagh had not been a convinced abolitionist, and he had
looked upon the campaign as sentimental. His conversion to the
view that the traffic must be ended was sincere, however, and not
just the result of public opinion. Even Wilberforce, the leader
of the abolition movement, said that he had 'no suspicion of
Castlereagh'. There were really two separate difficulties in ending

the slave trade. First there was the need to secure the agreement to abolition of the nations involved in it. Secondly there was the problem of how to enforce such an agreement. With the former, Castlereagh was successful, although in the case of Spain and Portugal not without large cash payments, unceasing diplomatic pressure and threats of sanctions and boycott. Prevention was more difficult to secure. The only chance of full prevention lay in all countries actively as well as passively supporting the ban; at the same time there was a need for some form of policing at sea. In both France and the United States there were strong bodies of opinion against abolition, in the case of France because it was associated with the occupying powers. Both the United States and France resisted the British wish that her navy—the only one capable of adequate policing—should have the right to visit and search suspect ships, even if they flew national flags. Thus despite his efforts, Castlereagh's attempts were only partly successful, but certainly his role cannot be seen as reactionary.

In the final account perhaps Lord Salisbury was correct to suggest, when writing of Castlereagh's reputation, that he 'might have maintained his policy with impunity if in his speeches he would have done readier homage to the Liberal catchwords of the day. If he had only constructed a few brilliant periods about nationality or freedom, or given a little wordy sympathy to Greece, or Naples, or Spain, or the South American republics, the world would have heard much less of the horrors of his policy.'

3 International government or national interest It was not only as a reactionary that Castlereagh was attacked by writers in the nineteenth century. He was execrated as the dupe of other powers, one who had sacrificed British interests to the advantage of others. The diarist Greville wrote: 'I believe that he was seduced by his vanity, that his head was turned by emperors, kings and congresses . . .' His actions after 1815 were abused as those of a pawn of Metternich, either unwitting and misled or deliberate and treasonable. His attachment to congresses of the major powers and meetings with foreign statesmen was seen as symptomatic of this, while his American policy was attacked as pusillanimous.

This view was only tenable at a time when Castlereagh's work was not properly studied. The French historian Sorel knew better; writing of Castlereagh's principles he claimed that they 'were in no measure abstract or speculative; they were all comprehended in one, the supremacy of English interests'. No recent historian has attacked Castlereagh as lacking in a proper regard for the interest of his country. If the problems he had to face after 1815 and the steps he took to solve them are examined, it becomes clear that national interest was always his overriding objective, whatever his methods of achieving it.

In Britain's dealings with the United States, where he was criticised for lack of firmness, Castlereagh wished, in his own words, 'to regulate our intercourse in all respects as that each Nation may be able to do its utmost towards making the other rich and happy'. He believed that whatever temporary disagreements there might be, the basic interest of both countries was mutual peace—as at the time a third of all the United States' imports came from Britain, it is difficult to controvert his belief. Nevertheless the causes of disagreement were very real and bitterly felt, and there could have been a prolongation of the 1812–14 war or renewed outbreaks following the peace. Castlereagh's policy was explained in a phrase he used to an American diplomat: 'Time will do more than we can.'

The Peace of Ghent, signed by Britain and the United States in 1814, justified the attack made upon it in the House of Commons: 'There is no one subject whatever that existed in dispute between the two countries that does not in fact still exist.' No solution was attempted to the burning issue of Britain's maritime rights with respect to American ships, nor was the Canadian frontier with America finally settled; it could not have been without a quarrel. Instead Castlereagh succeeded in obtaining some reduction in the construction of warships by both sides on the Great Lakes. More significant, perhaps, was the incident in 1818 when an American general, Andrew Jackson, invaded Spanish Florida and executed two British subjects for being involved in Indian raids into American territory. Despite demands for war, echoed and magnified in the press, Castlereagh held firm to conciliation, although, as he told the American ambassador, 'War might have been produced by holding up a finger.' In these cases Castlereagh felt that with the passage of time the disputes would be forgotten. His dealings with the United States cannot be better summed up than by Sir Charles Webster: 'All that he did was done so unobtrusively and with such little desire to enhance his own reputation that it obtained the obscurity necessary for success.'

Another problem that confronted Castlereagh in the New World arose from the successful revolt of Spain's former colonies. Britain was, of course, a colonial power herself, and certainly could not with equanimity side with republican rebels against their king. On the other hand, Britain had increasingly important trade relations with South America and had no wish to see the United States develop their influence in that region, as they might do by appearing the only friend of the new states and granting them full diplomatic recognition. Castlereagh's policy was to work for an agreement between Spain and her former colonies. Force should not be employed against the colonies, whether Spanish, French, or even Russian, and Britain with her command of the seas was able in the last resort to enforce such a decision. At the same time Britain sought to avoid the need for such extreme measures by dissuading France and Russia, in the name of the Alliance, from pursuing independent policies. Britain also employed the Alliance as a threat to restrain the United States from a quick diplomatic recognition of the rebel colonies, with the suggestion that if she acted she would find the European powers against her.

Although he never abandoned hope of an agreement, Castlereagh came to see it as less likely, and worked at least to try to ensure that the new states should be monarchies rather than republics: 'There are already enough republican ideas in the world; to increase the sum of these ideas is to compromise more and more the fate of monarchy in Europe.' The situation at sea, where ships that traded with the colonies were treated by the Spanish as pirates, had become insufferable to British merchants;

it was this which prompted Castlereagh to give what amounted to commercial recognition to the rebel colonies. Nevertheless he still looked to a negotiated peace as the best solution and planned further discussions at the Congress of Verona, which he was about to attend when he died in the summer of 1822.

But of course the most important part of Castlereagh's foreign policy, after as before 1815, was his handling of European problems. Here again Castlereagh's main object was to secure peace. His experience of the price that had been paid to obtain concord helps to explain the Foreign Secretary's anxiety to preserve it. In the years after 1815 France remained the preoccupation of the victors, and a Congress held in 1818 was primarily concerned with French affairs. The Second Peace of Paris had left unresolved the size of private damages which France was to pay for injuries caused by her troops. Also it had been decided that the period of occupation by the victorious armies should be five years with the possibility of a reduction to three. In pursuit of the policy of moderation the British government wished to lessen the burdens upon France. Wellington had previously recommended a reduction in the size of the army of occupation and now Britain wanted to withdraw it altogether. It was to discuss these matters that a conference of the allies met at Aix-la-Chapelle at the end of September 1818, and because of the subjects for discussion it was natural to invite the French to take part. The Congress ratified financial provisions already agreed upon and went on to wind up the occupation of France.

It was at this stage that differences appeared. One reason why Castlereagh had been anxious to hold the Congress was his fear that Russia might be contemplating an independent policy of alliance with France, and a meeting of all the allies seemed the best way of preventing this. In his own words: 'Placed as the Cabinets now are side by side to each other, misconceptions have been immediately obviated and a divergence of opinion is likely to be avoided.' Nevertheless the Tsar attempted to bring France into a general alliance—an *Alliance Solidaire*—which was to guarantee the thrones and the territories of all sovereigns. This was the scheme the Tsar had brought forward in 1815, and it was now even less palatable to Castlereagh than it had been then. As he wrote: 'The problem of an universal Alliance for the peace and happiness of the world, has always been one of speculation and of hope, but it has never yet been reduced to practice, and if an opinion may be hazarded from its difficulties, it never can . . . Till, then, a system of administering Europe by a general Alliance of all its states can be reduced to some practical form, all notions of general and unqualified guarantee must be abandoned.' However, a straight refusal might well have encouraged Russia to deal directly with France, and in this way destroy the alliance Castlereagh did wish to preserve, the Quadruple Alliance. A solution was found by inviting France to join the concert of powers, and she signed a declaration together with the other major powers which assumed French participation in future gatherings. As a result of this the Tsar was prepared to take part in a secret renewal of the Quadruple Alliance. In Castlereagh's words: 'The expedient is then to give France her concert but to keep our security.' Although the Congress ended in apparent amity it had demonstrated that Castlereagh's ideas of the way forward were not the same as the Tsar's and that he was not prepared to acquiesce in policies not in Britain's interests. At the same time, although Castlereagh seemed to have been successful, the effort of allowing France back into the concert was to undermine the Quadruple Alliance, which, to the British people, could only be a mechanism to control France.

The issue that was eventually to lead to the break between Britain and her allies was the future of the Iberian peninsula. Both Spain and Portugal found themselves with unsatisfactory and incapable rulers at the conclusion of the Napoleonic Wars. John, Regent and then—after his mother's death in 1816—King of Portugal, had been living in the Portuguese colony of Brazil since 1807 and so added non-residence to his incompetence. Ferdinand VII of Spain, for his part, was seemingly unaware of the problems he faced and blind to the real condition of his kingdom.

In January 1820 revolt broke out among troops assembling at Cadiz prior to an attempt to recapture Ferdinand's rebellious colonies in the New World. It spread, and in March Ferdinand was forced to accept the very democratic constitution which Spain had briefly enjoyed—or suffered—on liberation from France in 1812. Even before the constitution was granted Russia was beginning a diplomatic offensive against the revolt and was in favour of outside action to check it.

Naturally Alexander urged repression in the name of the European states, the *Alliance Solidaire* which he had already proposed. Such action was opposed to British interests and Castlereagh was adamant against it. Events in Spain, as he wrote in his state paper of 1820, did not appear to 'menace other states with that imminent danger which had always been regarded, at least in this country, as alone constituting the case which would justify external interference'. Russian action would mean interference and a dramatic and unwanted increase in Russian power in an area where Britain regarded herself as particularly involved. If French troops were used, geographically and physically the most probable course, it meant the establishment of French influence in Spain and possibly the formation of the Franco-Russian alliance which Britain had determinedly opposed. Finally, if intervention was to be through the Alliance by a combined military force, Britain and Castlereagh would find themselves unable to acquiesce. In the important state paper which set out Britain's objections Castlereagh affirmed: 'It [the Alliance] never was . . . intended as an union for the government of the world or for the superintendence of the internal affairs of other States . . . this country cannot and will not act upon abstract and speculative principles of caution. The Alliance which exists had no such purpose in view in its original formation.' Castlereagh refused Russian requests for a congress to discuss Spanish affairs and instead worked through Metternich, who, while having no sympathy for the Spanish revolutionaries, was opposed to a Franco-Russian alliance or any increase in Russian power in Western Europe. Together Castlereagh and Metternich were able to negate Russian policies, and until his death Castlereagh was to continue to follow these tactics in the face of mounting chaos in Spain.

He did not, however, favour the Spanish revolution, and warned the constitutional government against political extremism and particularly against interfering in Portugal, 'either by tampering with his (the Portuguese King's) troops or subjects or by inviting or accepting the defection of his people'. Britain had a direct treaty obligation to Portugal and important trading interests as well; therefore she was totally against any outside interference when constitutional troubles overtook the country. In 1820, however, revolt in Naples faced Castlereagh with a different situation, one that could not be solved by working with the Austrian Chancellor. When the King of Naples was forced to grant a constitution in the face of rebellion, Metternich, believing that Italian affairs affected Austria directly, and already alarmed by disturbances in the German Confederation, was determined to act. He feared, however, that Russia and France might try to counter Austrian action by posing as the protectors of Italy's rights. He was therefore concerned to gain French and Russian approval for Austrian intervention while not wishing them to participate physically in such an enterprise.

If Austrian troops had marched into Naples and restored Ferdinand to his former position there would have been no objection from Castlereagh; he even counselled speed to the Austrians. But he strongly objected to such action being carried out in the name of an alliance of which Britain was a member. He did not attend the Congress at Troppau in 1820 nor when it was reconvened at Laibach early in 1821, since the Italian problem was the subject for discussion and Castlereagh refused to accept that this was a problem for the Alliance. However, he did agree to the attendance of his half-brother, Lord Stewart, as an observer, and because of the latter's gullibility Britain seemed to be more closely associated with the decisions of the Congress than Castlereagh wished. Particularly was this so with the Troppau Protocol, which set out the principle that states which underwent changes in their constitutions because of revolution would cease to belong to the European Alliance if the changes seemed dangerous to other states. In this case measures would be taken to bring the states back to 'the bosom of the Alliance'. These measures would be 'first friendly representations, secondly measures of coercion'.

This embarrassed Castlereagh to the extent that he felt it necessary to state his attitude in a circular sent to all British representatives at foreign courts. In this Castlereagh stated that the British Government 'do not regard the Alliance as entitled, under existing Treaties, to assume, in their character as allies, any such general powers, nor do they conceive that such extra-ordinary powers could be assumed, . . . amongst the Allied Courts, without their . . . attributing to themselves a supremacy incompatible with the rights of other States.'

It is sometimes argued that this statement was the product of the parliamentary weakness of the Tory government and Castle-reagh's need to appease critics in the House of Commons. The Austrian ambassador reported: 'Castlereagh is like a great lover of music who is at church; he wishes to applaud but he dares not.' Certainly the weakness of the government did affect Castle-reagh, but primarily in that it lessened his influence over the leaders of other states who were aware that he might lose office. 'They [Austria, Prussia and Russia] idly persevere in attributing the line we have taken and must steadily continue to take to the temporary difficulties in which the government has been placed, instead of imputing them to those principles which in our system must be immutable . . .' was Castlereagh's comment. The Foreign Secretary's circular accords with his previous reactions to pro-posals for collective intervention by the Alliance in other states, and seems to stem from his refusal of an *Alliance Solidaire* rather than to spring from political expediency or from the force of necessity.

Even so, Castlereagh was still trying to work with the Alliance, as he demonstrated at the time of the Greek revolt against the Turkish Sultan. An attempt at revolution in the Danubian Principalities by some Greeks had failed, but had led to a rising in the Morea, in Greece itself. There were strong reasons why the Tsar Alexander should intervene on the side of the Greeks. First they were his co-religionists rebelling against a Muslim ruler; secondly Alexander was advised by Capo d'Istria, who came from the island of Corfu and was eager for Greek independence; finally war against Turkey was a traditional policy of Russia and offered opportunity for territorial gain. Castlereagh, like Metternich, was alarmed at the instability of the Near East and feared Russian power there following a Turkish collapse. At once he wrote to the Tsar and also sought to work through Metternich to restrain him. National interest was threatened, so Castlereagh threw his efforts into renewing the Alliance, which had seemed at breaking-point.

Castlereagh did not seek to crush the Greek revolt, although he had little sympathy for its aims. His preoccupation was with the possibility of a Russo-Turkish war, and it was to avoid this eventuality that the British and Austrian Ministers worked. They sought to persuade Alexander that action on his part endangered the Alliance, and tried to forward negotiations between Turkish and Russian diplomats, extracting some concessions from the Turks without driving them into a position of desperation from which they would look to war for release.

Castlereagh's co-operation with Metternich was greatly facilitated by a journey he made with George IV to Hanover in the autumn of 1821. It was because of a meeting there with Metternich that Castlereagh agreed to try to attend the Congress that was to be held the following year. This had originally been planned to wind up the affairs of Italy, where a revolution in Piedmont had followed the Austrian army's success in Naples. It was also clear that Spain would feature in the discussion: the situation was deteriorating, and the emergence of a new government in France had made intervention more likely. It was the Greek revolt, however, which persuaded Castlereagh that British participation was essential at the Congress, as the Alliance was the only instrument that could be employed for peace.

It was a Congress that Castlereagh was not after all to attend. Whether from overwork in a long and hectic parliamentary session, the constant worry over the affairs of Europe or a persecution mania that was brought on by blackmail it is hard to say, but in August of 1822 Castlereagh had lost his usual calm composure and his manner alarmed both the Duke of Wellington and the

King. His spirit shattered, he committed suicide at his country house in Kent on 12 August.

His death meant that at the Congress of Verona Metternich lacked a firm ally in dealing with Spain and the Greek revolt. The Chancellor had already feared that to continue to restrain Russia from action against the Turks some sort of declaration of solidarity might be necessary from the powers—one that Castlereagh would have had no wish to sign. As it was, without an ally, Metternich was forced to go much further and had to accept French intervention in Spain on behalf of the King. What happened at Verona, therefore, cannot fairly be accepted as evidence for the failure of Castlereagh's schemes.

4 The unanswered questions   That national interest inspired Castlereagh's policies there is not now much doubt. There are, however, two related areas of his foreign policy where disagreement exists, first as to the extent of Castlereagh's involvement in the 'Congress System', and secondly as to whether his policy was still viable by the time of his death.

After the First World War, when, determined that there should be no more wars, men turned to international government as the solution to their problems, their view of the past was changed. Whereas in nineteenth-century Britain nationalism had been approved and even glorified, it was now looked upon as an important cause of war and disaster. A foreign policy pursued in concert with other powers was no longer thought craven, but was admired as high-minded. Thus it was not surprising that Castlereagh's belief in an alliance of the major European powers, grouped together not for war, but to avoid war, was seen as praiseworthy. It is typical of this change in attitude that the Foreign Office's lack of a portrait of Castlereagh should only have been felt in 1925. For 1925 was the year of the Treaty of Locarno, of hope that European states at last were coming to order their affairs through discussion rather than war. Hence a portrait of Castlereagh was borrowed by the Foreign Office in that year, before the European statesmen arrived in London for the formal signature of the Treaty.

It was natural, particularly in the climate of internationalism which prevailed after 1918, that great emphasis should have been placed on the periodic gatherings of statesmen provided for in Article Six of the Quadruple Alliance of 1815. This article had declared: 'To facilitate and to secure the execution of the present Treaty, and to consolidate the connections which at the present moment so closely unite the four Sovereigns for the happiness of the world, the High Contracting Parties have agreed to renew their meetings at fixed periods . . . for the purpose of consulting upon their common interests, and for the consideration of the measures which at each of these periods shall be considered the most salutary for the repose and prosperity of Nations and for the maintenance of the peace of Europe.' As the author of this Article, Castlereagh has sometimes been portrayed as the architect of a totally new method of transacting international relations, described as the Congress System, and depicted as a premature Security Council of the United Nations. More recently, however, historians have questioned this interpretation. The most extreme example is perhaps L. C. B. Seaman, who, in *Vienna to Versailles*, dismisses the notion of a Congress System as the invention of historians. He and others have pointed out that there was no permanent organisation or secretariat created, and that no attempt was made to arrange the frequency of meetings. Above all, only four reunions occurred, of which Castlereagh attended just one. This, it is argued, hardly suggests that the British Foreign Secretary based his policy on a Congress System.

Other writers, for example H. Kissinger and C. J. Bartlett, have not totally discounted the Congresses but have doubted whether their role was crucial. Bartlett argued that what was really of importance to Castlereagh was diplomacy based upon personal contact, and that in furthering this the Congresses had a part to play though they were never at the centre of his policy. It is interesting in the light of this to read Castlereagh's instruction to a newly appointed British Minister to the United States: 'To transact your business with the American Government as far as possible by personal intercourse with the Secretary of State rather than by written notes, thereby avoiding . . . diplomatic controversy'. Castlereagh's rebuff to the Tsar's request for a Congress on Spanish affairs in 1820 is indicative of the limited role he wished the 'periodic gatherings' to play. In his refusal he deprecated the attitude 'that whenever any great political event shall occur, as in Spain . . . it is to be regarded almost as a matter of course, that it belongs to the Allies to charge themselves collectively with the responsibility of exercising some jurisdiction concerning . . . possible eventual danger'.

The basis of Castlereagh's policy was the Quadruple Alliance. This was a means of repelling danger to Europe, particularly from a France that might be torn again by revolution and led by a new Napoleon. This Alliance had no business in the domestic crises of others, in Spain, in Portugal or in Naples, but it was concerned to prevent a·war between Russia and Turkey. Castlereagh himself wrote in 1816: 'Such an Alliance could only have owed its origin to a sense of common danger; in its very nature it must be conservative; it cannot threaten either the security or the liberties of other States.' His great achievement lay in perceiving that Britain could better secure her interests acting through the other powers than against them. His failure was that he could not explain this, not to the country, not to Parliament, often not even to his Cabinet colleagues.

Although the importance which Castlereagh attached to the Congresses will always be difficult to measure, recent writers have carried conviction in their assertions that in the past it has often been exaggerated. To the other question, however, whether Castlereagh's policies would have continued to be fruitful if he had lived longer, there can never be a final answer. One view, the older, holds that by 1822 it was no longer possible for Britain to work through the Alliance to forward her interests. Since France had been accepted by the other powers the Alliance had lost its purpose, and British public opinion was becoming increasingly restive as the Foreign Secretary continued to maintain close relations with the autocratic monarchies of Eastern Europe. The Alliance would have become progressively more reactionary and thus unsuitable for a constitutional monarchy such as Britain.

Because of this even Webster saw Castlereagh's policy as bankrupt by 1822.

The other, more recent, view holds that failure was not inevitable. It is argued that although Castlereagh might have encountered unpopularity through his policies this was unlikely to have prevented him from pursuing them. He was well used to being unpopular and his position in 1822 was so strong that it is difficult to see how he could have been forced from office. At the same time it is by no means certain that his policies of co-operation were doomed to failure. Metternich's inability to prevent French intervention in Spain is hardly proof that with Castlereagh's assistance and working through the Alliance he would still have failed. Certainly Canning's policy was unsuccessful later in checking French action. It is also significant that Canning resorted to the expedient of siding with Russia and France in order to try to restrain them in the Near East. The situation in the Near East, which was to become so important during the 1820s, is in fact an interesting piece of evidence against the view that Britain would necessarily find herself increasingly isolated from her autocratic allies in the Alliance as time passed.

Castlereagh had favoured international co-operation in the first instance because it was vital in the war with Napoleon that Britain should secure the assistance of the Continental powers. His experience in Europe in 1814 had taught him how difficult it was to maintain a Grand Alliance and how critical was Britain's role if any such alliance was to be achieved. He came to see that by acting in concert with other powers Britain could exert a force for stability. Events in 1814 demonstrated that Castlereagh was able to hold the alliance together, and led him to believe that he would be able to do so in future. Whether he was right or wrong in his belief must remain an open question.

Chapter IV

Canning

1 The man and his ideas George Canning's origins and boyhood were romantic and for a future Prime Minister somewhat bizarre, but as an adult his domestic life was tranquil, with contented family circumstances and an absence of emotional intrigues and *affaires*. His father, of a literary and radical bent, was the disinherited son of a prosperous Ulsterman; his mother was an indigent, if well-born, beauty. Soon widowed, Canning's mother sought her future as a touring actress and took up with an actor to whom she bore several children before re-marrying. Canning, now in the care of his father's brother, had a modest income settled on him by his grandfather and was educated at Eton and Oxford, where, brilliantly successful, he soon attracted notice.

Patronised by the Prime Minister, William Pitt, Canning was found a seat in Parliament at the age of twenty-three, held junior office in 1796, and by 1800 was a Privy Councillor and married to a lady of means. He resigned from office with Pitt in 1801 and thereafter remained a firm advocate of Catholic emancipation. He joined the Cabinet as Foreign Secretary in 1807, holding office for two years before he resigned over the dispute with Castlereagh which led to their duel. He was hampered in regaining office by his assumption that he was indispensable, a trait which led him to impose impossible conditions for his return.

For example, in 1812 he was offered the Foreign Office, Castlereagh agreeing to give up the post and retain the Leadership of the House of Commons. However, Canning felt unable to serve under Castlereagh as Leader, 'not from any personal feeling towards Castlereagh . . . but from a sense of humiliation—hard to endure and I think unnecessary to be proposed to me'. Canning was sent as ambassador to Lisbon in 1814, in anticipation of the Portuguese king's return from Brazil, but it was not until 1816 that he entered the government as President of the Board of Control. He resigned once more in 1820, this time over the Queen's divorce, a gesture which increased George IV's dislike. Canning's support for Queen Caroline was based upon their previous friendship; some even alleged that before his marriage the two had been lovers.

The opportunity came to go to India as Governor-General, but Castlereagh's death intervened and Canning, delaying his departure, received Castlereagh's office. Finally, in 1827, strongly opposed by the reactionary Tories, he formed his own government; the King now supported his popular policy and was his firmest advocate. His health, already broken by strain and overwork, rallied briefly, but in August he died.

Canning's ambitions and his belief in himself are revealed in the story of his life. It is also easy to see why he was considered an *arriviste*. One contemporary claimed that Canning 'considers politics as a game and has no idea of any regard to principle interfering with his object of getting to power'. Certainly many in Parliament thought him untrustworthy and unprincipled, with the result that he was always at pains to demonstrate the falsity of this view. His origins and his mother's career were scorned and used as explanations for his disingenuousness but were not in themselves the reason for suspicion. Croker believed that Canning 'could hardly have tea without a stratagem', and Brougham saw him as 'an actor . . . a first rate one no doubt—but still an actor'. No one questioned Canning's financial probity but many were worried by his single-minded ambition for political power and position. 'Yet still the desire for fame . . . drives me back to public affairs', he wrote.

Along with his determination to succeed, the two qualities which stand out in Canning are his extreme intelligence and his enormous industry. The best known example of his speed of mind comes from Greville. 'He [Canning] could not bear to dictate, because nobody could write fast enough for him; but on one occasion, when he had the gout in his hand and could not write, he stood by the fire and dictated at the same time a despatch on Greek affairs to George Bentinck and one on South American politics to Howard de Walden, each writing as fast as he could, while he turned from one to the other without hesitation or embarrassment.' Canning had the ability to master a subject and to marshal a superbly lucid argument. Since he also had a wounding wit which he used unrestrainedly, Canning was a formidable debater and a writer of trenchant despatches. With his swift intelligence allied to voracity for work—'the happiness of constant occupation is infinite', he claimed—it is no wonder that he kept Lord Liverpool busy. 'I live in continual dread every time the door opens that it is to bring a note from Mr Canning, till I am driven half-distracted', wrote the Prime Minister.

A brilliant speaker, a derisive wit, suspected of being unprincipled; in these respects Canning is a contrast with Castlereagh, although the capacity for work was certainly common to both. How similar were their foreign policies? Certainly Canning had questioned Castlereagh's attachment to the Congresses. A Cabinet colleague wrote of Canning's views: 'He thinks that system of periodical meetings of the four great Powers, with a view to the general concerns of Europe, new and of very questionable policy; that it will necessarily involve us deeply in all the politics of the Continent, whereas our true policy has always been not to interfere except in great emergencies, and then with commanding force.' At the same time Canning made more parade than his predecessor of the national interest which determined his policy: 'I hope that I have as friendly disposition towards the nations of the earth, as anyone who vaunts his philanthropy most highly; but I am contented to confess, that in the conduct of political affairs, the grand object of my contemplation is the interest of England.' This concentration on the

'Englishness' of his policy in numerous speeches, his obvious relish at the disengagement of England from what he saw as the system of Congresses and alliance, together with his openly displayed dislike for Metternich, have led some writers to separate his policy from Castlereagh's.

In sharp contrast to Castlereagh was Canning's style of conducting his policy. Temperley wrote: 'In Canning's view, it was essential that future foreign policy should be both intelligible and popular.' He sought with success to explain to the country what he was doing, and in return received assent and approbation. Some, with Metternich, saw this departure as 'a pretension that is misplaced in a statesman'. Mrs Arbuthnot, wife of a Tory politician and admirer of Castlereagh, claimed that Canning's attempts at 'going round the country speechifying and discussing the Acts and intentions of the Gov't were ridiculous' and 'quite a new system *among us* . . . [one which] excites great indignation'.

Whether this difference of style was so great as to amount to a change of policy will become clearer as Canning's policies and actions are examined. What must be accepted is that because Canning was neither really known nor trusted by other European leaders, however much he might have wanted to follow Castlereagh he had no hope of working through the same personal contacts. The relationships which Castlereagh had developed with European statesmen were the product partly of his personality, partly of circumstance. Canning had a very different personality and had not shared the same circumstances. In fact Canning mistrusted the close relationships of Castlereagh with foreign statesmen and was not even prepared to try to maintain them. There would not only be differences in technique between the two men, but the differences would be self-proclaimed.

2 Worlds old and new Although at the time they were closely interrelated it is helpful to try to separate the problems that faced Canning in Spain, in Portugal and in the New World. In Spain the constitutional regime had proved chaotic and incapable, while the King, chafing under his parliament and his ministers, sought to obtain foreign assistance to overthrow the constitution and regain his former autocratic powers. The attempt to prevent such intervention was one that Canning inherited from Castlereagh; Cunning, through Wellington at the Congress of Verona, refused to join in any common policy against Spain and attempted to dissuade France from intervention by personal diplomatic activity. Despite early confidence, however, he failed, and April 1823 brought the French invasion of Spain, the speedy defeat of the constitutional government and the restoration of Ferdinand's powers. Although determined to eschew Castlereagh's policies of working through Metternich to prevent the invasion of Spain, Canning had found no alternative way of proceeding. Should he merely acquiesce belatedly in the *fait accompli*?

First he was faced with the fear that the French invaders, or the Spanish backed by the French, might be tempted to involve themselves in Portugal, a state to which Britain was obliged by alliance and which was undergoing its own constitutional troubles. Secondly there was the possibility that France would assist Ferdinand to regain his colonies in the New World, or even try to capture some part of them for herself. Thirdly, and very important though less easy to demonstrate, was the shock to British prestige of the French invasion of Spain and the continued presence of French troops in an area from which Britain had spent six years in expelling them during the Peninsular War.

'Portugal has been, and always *must* be English, so long as Europe and the world remain in anything like their present state', wrote Canning at this time. Before French troops had crossed the frontier into Spain Canning had made it clear that British neutrality depended upon there being no interference with Portugal. Meanwhile he warned the Portuguese against any provocative action. He maintained his tough line, sending a naval squadron to the Tagus, securing the recall of a French ambassador in Lisbon who seemed to be too involved in Portuguese politics, and finally, in 1826, following incursions from Spanish-based Portuguese rebels, despatching British troops to Portugal. Canning told the House of Commons: 'We go to Portugal . . . to defend and preserve the independence of an Ally.' Canning also acted firmly to prevent French assistance being given to Spain in the New World. Choosing a time when France was pre-occupied with the Spanish campaign, he demanded and received written assurance that no such action would be taken or contemplated.

Canning believed that after French intervention in Spain it was important to restore British prestige. He was to rely upon his tough actions over Portugal as one way of demonstrating that Britain had not abdicated her position in the Iberian Peninsula, but he also tried to repair the damage by his speeches. 'I resolved that if France had Spain, it should not be Spain with the Indies. I called the New World into existence to redress the balance of the Old', he told Parliament; and in a speech at Plymouth soon after he received news of the French victory in Spain he demanded, 'Let it not be said that we cultivate peace, either because we fear, or because we are unprepared for, war.'

The difficulties which Canning faced over the affairs of Portugal stemmed from her constitutional instability and her relations with Brazil. The return of King John from Brazil to Portugal in 1821 and his acceptance of the new constitution were followed by a revolution in Brazil in which John's eldest son, Dom Pedro, was proclaimed Emperor. After considerable reluctance and prevarication Portugal finally agreed to allow Britain to mediate, and in 1825 recognised the Brazilian Empire as independent. This result was a considerable triumph for Canning, because British interests had been safeguarded and the new state, as he had desired, was a monarchy.

Instability within Portugal continued, endangering Britain chiefly because it invited foreign interference. The Queen, aided by her second son Dom Miguel, refused to accept the constitution and tried to force the King to restore the Ultras to power. After King John's death in 1826 Dom Pedro chose to remain in Brazil and waived his claims in favour of his daughter, Donna Maria, who he proposed should marry her uncle, Dom Miguel. The situation remained dangerously unsettled, but at least Canning was able to prevent overt foreign interference and lessen the risk of division in Portugal giving opportunities for foreign intervention.

In the New World, Canning followed much the same aims as Castlereagh, trying to protect British trade while working for a negotiated settlement between Spain and her rebellious colonies, and still hoping that some of them would emerge as monarchies. At the same time Canning tried to prevent the United States from becoming excessively influential in Latin America. He attempted to work in concert with the United States, but was unable to agree to the condition of immediate full recognition of the ex-colonies. There followed the message of the United States President to Congress—the Monroe Doctrine—at the end of 1823 which laid down the principle of non-interference by European powers with the independent states of the Americas. Although excluding colonies of European states it expressly included former colonies now diplomatically recognised by the United States. This might have seemed to seize the initiative in Latin America for the United States, but Canning carried conviction in arguing that it was the British Navy alone which could physically protect Latin America from Europe, whatever the United States might proclaim. The Latin American leader Bolivar recognised this when he remarked that 'only England, mistress of the seas, can protect us against the united forces of European reaction'. At the same time Canning used the fear of the growing influence of the United States to stifle Cabinet objections to full recognition for Buenos Aires, Mexico and Colombia, formally proclaimed in February 1825.

'Looking to the recognition of the independence of the South American states—looking to the succours that had been sent to Portugal— . . . no three preceding years could be compared with the three which had elapsed [1824-7] . . . in point of brilliant, beneficial, and successful policy', claimed one M.P. Canning had shrugged off his early failure in Spain; he had safeguarded Britain's interests and won her unprecedented prestige and admiration abroad.

The essence of the charge against Canning in these matters is that he was primarily concerned with showy self-dramatisation. In playing and winning a hand that was virtually unloseable, Canning in the eyes of one historian 'converted a routine operation into a splendid publicity campaign'. He may have gained friends and won prestige in South America, but it was economic reality rather than political sentiment which led to the increase of Britain's trade with that area in the following period. In his somewhat tactless and overbearing handling of the United States, Canning never succeeded in really winning trust, and certainly British-American relations improved markedly following his death. Castlereagh had a clearer appreciation of the need to maintain friendship with the United States and of the sacrifices necessary to do so.

3 The Eastern question and the making of Greece   Tsar Alexander's refusal to help the Greek insurgents who were trying to prise the Danubian Principalities from the grasp of the Sultan had spelt their failure. The rising in the Morea was something very different. From the outset, despite bitter rivalry among the revolutionaries, the Turks found the revolt extremely difficult to suppress. As command of the sea was with the Greeks, Turkish troops and supplies had to travel overland from Constantinople and were highly vulnerable to guerilla warfare. The revolt extended north of the Gulf of Corinth and many of the Greek islands renounced Turkish rule.

Although both sides were soon notorious for the bestiality of their reprisals and counter-reprisals, it was Turkish acts, such as the massacre of the inhabitants of Chios and the hanging of the Patriarch of Constantinople that really scandalised European opinion. Russian anger was whipped up to a point where a resumption of chronic Russo-Turkish hostilities seemed inevitable, and the policy of Castlereagh and Metternich, that of persuading Alexander that the Greek rebellion must be treated as a rebellion and not the excuse for a crusade, was rendered almost impossible. For their part, the Turks saw the hand of the Tsar in the revolt and made no secret of their antagonism. Thus the departure of the Russian ambassador from Constantinople and the subsequent breaking-off of diplomatic relations came as no surprise.

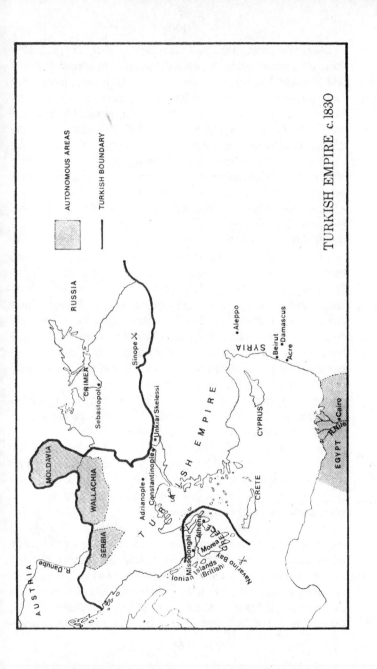

TURKISH EMPIRE c.1830

AUTONOMOUS AREAS

TURKISH BOUNDARY

Canning's succession to Castlereagh's office did not alter Britain's determination to prevent Russia from unilateral action which might lead to the collapse of the Ottoman Empire, but Canning was less willing and less able to work through Metternich to inhibit such Russian action. The immediate problem which the Greek revolt posed for Canning, however, was the danger to British commerce in the Aegean arising from the Greco-Turkish hostilities there. Canning, faced otherwise with treating the Greeks as pirates, chose in 1823 to recognise them as belligerents, a decision in fact which had been in Castlereagh's mind a year earlier. In Canning's own words: 'Belligerency was not so much a principle as a fact.' Nevertheless to some his action implied the acceptance of revolution.

The more fundamental danger which confronted Canning, that of a Russo-Turkish war, was unaffected by his decision. He worked to separate the Greek revolt from the quarrel between Russia and Turkey because their confusion made Russian action more likely. To this end the English ambassador at Constantinople sought to restore diplomatic relations between the two Powers, and by 1823 his efforts seemed to be successful. If Russo-Turkish hostility could be banked down Canning hoped the revolt might come to an end. On the one hand the Turks might suppress it, or on the other, the Sultan might if he believed victory impossible grant limited autonomy to the Greeks. Thus the seeming détente between Russia and Turkey promised well.

But Canning's hopes were to be dashed. The failure of the Turks to deal speedily with the revolt had given the Greeks time to attract sympathy to their cause. They were not just another people trying to win self-rule; a classically educated Europe knew what Shelley meant when he wrote, 'We are all Greeks.' Above all the decision of Byron to go to Greece and his death at Missolonghi in 1824 aroused popular support for the Greeks to a point where it would not have been easy for the British Foreign Secretary, particularly one who was as aware of public opinion as Canning, to stand aside and see them crushed. Meanwhile the Sultan showed that he was not prepared to accept defeat, and he secured the aid of Mehemet Ali, the Pasha of Egypt, and his son

Ibrahim. At once the maritime supremacy of the Greeks was challenged and their defeat became more likely.

The Tsar proved reluctant to settle his differences with Turkey and, looking for the authority to use force, he sought an international Congress. Metternich was prepared to accept a Congress as a way of stalling the Russians, but Canning opposed such a manoeuvre and refused British participation. During 1825 there were two important developments. First Alexander, seeing through Metternich's prevarication, became increasingly disenchanted, while his death at the end of the year, and the succession of his brother Nicholas, merely accelerated Russia's decision to follow her own line. Secondly Ibrahim, setting about the reconquest of Greece in a vigorous manner, reduced the Greeks to sending a deputation to London to beg Britain's help in their struggle.

Hence Canning was confronted with the necessity and the opportunity for a new initiative; the necessity because pressure grew for the government to save the Greeks, particularly when rumour spread that Ibrahim intended to depopulate the Morea and colonise it with Egyptians; necessity also because Russia seemed to be about to throw herself at Turkey. The opportunity came because, with the deterioration in her relations with Austria, Russia was more open to an approach from Britain. Canning had always contemplated co-operation with Russia—'to talk Greek with him [the Tsar] if he pleases'—provided Russia renounced the use of force and restored full relations with Turkey. The present crisis forced Canning to waive his conditions.

Canning had received word through the Russian ambassador, whose wife, Mme Lieven, returned with the news from a visit to Russia, that Alexander would consider friendly overtures from England. The death of Alexander made Canning more eager to act. The 'friendly overture' he adopted was to send the Duke of Wellington to St. Petersburg on a mission to congratulate Nicholas on his succession. The result of the Duke's discussions was a protocol signed in April 1826. Primarily this provided for mediation between Greece and Turkey on the basis of a virtually autonomous Greece which would pay tribute to the Sultan.

Russia continued meanwhile to press Turkey over other grievances and secured satisfaction in October at the Convention of Akkermann. After further successful diplomacy Canning was able to associate France with Britain and Russia in the Treaty of London of July 1827. This treaty was stronger than the Anglo-Russian protocol, demanding an immediate armistice, in default of which a secret article pledged the contracting parties to interpose themselves between the combatants.

Canning realised that this might lead to hostilities but pinned his hopes on an approach to Mehemet Ali, persuading him to recall his fleet and troops. This initiative failed in face of the Turks' refusal to accept an armistice. It was at this juncture that Canning died (August 1827), before the treaty was put to the test. The orders sent to the Admirals of Britain, France and Russia were extemely vague; it may be that if Canning had not been ill they would have been clearer. The ambiguity of the instructions was apparent to the British Admiral Codrington, upon whose actions the working of the treaty would depend. He questioned 'how we are by force to prevent the Turks . . . from pursuing any line of conduct which we are instructed to oppose, without committing hostility?'

The Turkish and Egyptian fleets were in the Greek harbour of Navarino when Codrington received his orders. Ibrahim asked permission on several occasions for his ships to be allowed to put to sea but was refused by the British admiral. Finally Codrington decided that the approach of winter made further blockade difficult. This was the reason for his decision to sail into Navarino harbour on 20 October to persuade the Egyptian fleet to return home. If not inviting a battle, Codrington was clearly hoping to force the issue. Fighting resulted, and by evening the Turkish and Egyptian fleets were destroyed.

In his speech from the throne King George IV was later to talk of Navarino as 'an untoward event' and refer to the Turks as 'an ancient ally'. But however contrary to the wishes of the British government the engagement was, Navarino meant that Greece would not now be reconquered, especially as French troops soon landed in the Morea and prepared to supervise the evacuation of

Egyptians and Turks. Turkish anger was particularly directed against Russia, and in the spring of 1828 war broke out, in fact over the interpretation of the Convention of Akkermann. The war did not result in the expected total destruction of Turkey, and it was not until the summer of 1829 that Russian troops reached Adrianople, where peace was signed, bringing Russian gains on the Danube. At the same time the Sultan was forced to accept Greece's independence, although her frontiers remained to be settled. These were not finally decided until 1832, when Prince Otto of Bavaria became the ruler of a completely independent Greek Kingdom.

Events in the Near East have been discussed in detail because it was here that Canning's most important work was accomplished. His policy in the New World and in connection with the Iberian Peninsula was obviously significant, but it was not really creative or imaginative in design, even if in execution it was original. It is to Canning's policy in the Near East that both his admirers and detractors first turn. What was he trying to do and was he successful? If his aim was to win Greece her freedom Canning may be accounted completely successful, and some in the past have claimed that he was pursuing this aim. He may have, in the words of Temperley, 'decided to protect Greece against Turkish oppression . . . contemplated her independence as possible' and it may be held that 'but for him there would have been no intervention'. But it seems that independence for the Greeks was never the primary objective of one who could write of them, 'There is no denying they are a most rascally set.'

The case for Canning is that his policy was a bold attempt to deal with the Eastern Question, a problem that was to continue to harass British statesmen throughout the nineteenth century. To work with Russia and seek to restrain her by co-operation was the one way the problem might have been solved. The rivalry with Russia and the long series of attempts—ultimately unsuccessful—to prop the sagging Turkish Empire could have been avoided. Instead, this chance of a forward-looking and constructive policy was thrown away by the bumbling ineptitude and timidity of Canning's successors, particularly the Duke of Wellington, who failed to comprehend the situation. The war between Russia and Turkey which followed Canning's death, for instance, was the outcome of Wellington's encouragement of the Turks.

A second view, while not denying the first, sees Canning particularly concerned with bringing about a diplomatic revolution. Britain was, by the early 1820s, faced with the choice between trailing along in the wake of an increasingly reactionary alliance which seemed to have little to offer her, and seeking her salvation alone. The years 1825-7 saw Canning destroy the old alliance and then create a new one in which Britain was at the centre rather than the periphery. 'In fact', writes R. J. V. Rolo, 'the Anglo-Russian alignment, which the Protocol implied, constituted a diplomatic revolution . . . From England's point of view Russia had become, in these spheres [Spain and Portugal] a benevolent neutral.'

Canning's detractors see his Near Eastern policy as either dangerously opportunist, or else as a noisy and unhelpful full circle back to the policy of Castlereagh. The latter view argues that what Canning was doing in 1825-7 was merely recreating a European Concert to deal with the Near East, something that Castlereagh and Metternich had always known to be necessary. Canning's policy was the outcome of his petty refusal to work with Metternich, whose prominence he resented.

'It was a fair comment of Metternich's on Canning's foreign policy in the East that he destroyed much and created nothing. His death enabled the Powers once more to co-operate', writes L. C. B. Seaman. Those who see Canning's policy as dangerous opportunism argue that his attempts to set Russia against Austria could only encourage the former to pursue a forward policy, something that would harm British interests. They ask what Canning would have done when Turkey and Russia finally went to war, since his colleagues would hardly have supported him in fighting the Turks. The fact that the war was not damaging to Britain was the outcome of Russian military weakness, something Canning had not counted on. His policy of trying to threaten Turkey without using force might have been fruitful with some states but was bound to lead to disaster with the Ottoman, who was inclined to fight even when reason counselled acquiescence.

In the last resort however, it will never be possible to judge Canning's policy with certainty for the simple reason that it cannot be known how he would have acted had he not died before Navarino.

4 New Liberal or new Tory 'If it can be said truly that Castlereagh inherited the repressive side of his great master, William Pitt, it is equally true to say that Canning carried on the earlier Pitt policy of progressive reform which had been lost in the whirlpools of the French Revolution.' This was the comparison made by Richard Aldington, a biographer of the Duke of Wellington, and however much the concept of Canning as a Liberal has been attacked a progressive redolence still flavours his reputation.

In his earliest days Canning favoured the Whigs, but abandoned them before entering Parliament. Save for his attachment to Catholic emancipation, which even Castlereagh supported, there is little sign of the Whig, far less the Liberal, in Canning's domestic policies. 'Jacobinism—*that* is the antagonism of Canning', thought one friend, and Canning himself wrote in 1823, 'Burke is still the manual of my politics.' His opposition to the reform of Parliament never wavered, and he fully supported the repressive actions in home affairs of the Tory government after 1815.

On the other hand Canning's period as Leader of the House of Commons and Foreign Secretary from 1822 to 1827 coincided with the period of change usually described as 'Liberal Toryism', and one of the exponents of reform, Huskisson, became a devoted disciple and colleague. Then when Canning finally became Prime Minister, Ultra-Tories such as Wellington and Eldon refused to serve under him. 'They who resist indiscriminately all improvements as innovations may find themselves compelled at last to submit to innovations although they are not improvements', was Canning's own judgement. Greville wrote: 'he was the only statesman who had the sagacity to enter into and comprehend the spirit of the times . . . The march of Liberalism . . . would not be

stopped . . . he resolved to . . . lead instead of opposing it.'
Michael Brock has argued that Canning was fighting to transform
the Tories into a party which could have continued in power for
many years, and that in refusing to accept him the Tory party
defeated itself. Others have merely seen him as an adventurer
pursuing power and donning what garb seemed to hold out
most promise of advantage at any particular moment.

However, it is on his foreign policy that Canning's reputation
as a progressive really rests. 'Though a member of a Tory
government . . . [Canning] was in foreign policy an exponent of
the new type of popular and liberal diplomacy' was the verdict of
H. A. L. Fisher. Was he? Canning's claim to have followed a
liberal foreign policy rests most upon his rôle of smiter of Metternich and the reactionary clique that were portrayed as governing
Europe. Canning's speech at the time of the French invasion of
Spain—'I earnestly hope and trust that she [Spain] may come
triumphantly out of the struggle', and his disregard for the
Congress System, taken together with his policies over Greece,
South America and Portugal mark him as a progressive. He
wrote to Lord Liverpool in 1824: 'Portugal appears to be the
chosen ground on which the Continental Alliance have resolved
to fight England hand to hand, and we must be prepared to meet
and defeat them, under every imaginable form of intrigue or
intimidation, or be driven from the field.' Metternich's own
freely expressed dislike for Canning and his policy further en-
deared him to liberals; someone whom the "High Priest" of
reaction saw as his enemy must be their friend. The Radical Sir
John Hobhouse expressed this view clearly: 'He [Canning] was no
friend of the people but circumstance had lately given him the
power and apparently the inclination, to be useful to the great
cause of public liberty . . . on the Continent, where I knew his
name was the terror of tyrants.'

Whatever the results of Canning's opposition to Metternich,
however, it is difficult not to attribute at least some of the cause to
personal dislike and jealousy. Metternich himself saw Canning as
motivated by malevolence rather than devotion to liberalism.
Certainly, except in those speeches and writings made with an

eye on the public, Canning did not suggest much love for some of the peoples and causes which assisted his policies. He referred to the constitutional party in Portugal as 'the scum of the earth . . . fierce, rascally, thieving, ignorant ragamuffins'; and he remarked to Mme. Lieven, talking of constitutional states, 'As a matter of taste, I should much prefer to do without them . . . The proof is that new America gives me a hundred times more trouble than old Europe.' Perhaps this message was intended to reach Metternich, but Canning expressed much the same sentiment when he said, 'Much better and more convenient for us to have neighbours, whose institutions cannot be compared with ours in point of freedom.'

It was perhaps the style of his policy and the attempt to make it popular that stamp Canning as so distinctively progressive. Some judges, contemporary as well as retrospective, have insisted that Canning's actions were primarily designed to win support for his own political position. In this way his frequent statements as to the Englishness of his aims as opposed to taking orders from Continental statesmen, while marking him as a progressive, were really designed to make him popular. Nevertheless, many historians have seen Canning as genuine in his protestations of English nationalism, however spurious his fame as a liberal may be. Algernon Cecil wrote: 'Combative, competitive and insular, he broadened a path for British policy.' One progressive and liberal policy that Canning pursued tirelessly and quite sincerely was his effort to end the slave trade. Temperley claims that 'his enthusiasm showed itself with a flame almost as fierce as . . . Wilberforce himself', and calculates that Canning wrote 'more than a thousand despatches over it'. Like Castlereagh, Canning inherited this cause from Pitt.

Perhaps the remark, made nearly a century and a half after Canning by the Marquis of Salisbury about the Conservative Minister Iain Macleod, 'Too clever by half', sums up one view of Canning's policies. These policies, neither those of a new Tory nor of a new Liberal, were the opportunism of a man who wanted power and believed that popularity would help him to attain it. To others Canning will remain, in the words of a recent biographer, R. J. V. Rolo, 'among the few who have successfully applied genius to politics'. Statesmen in this category have always found the English party system irksome, and party labels used to describe their political principles mislead rather than clarify.

Chapter V

Palmerston

1 The man and the legend Donald Southgate wrote in the introduction to his study of Palmerston, *The Most English Minister*, 'Palmerston must long await his true memorial. Unless a man of private means and single-minded devotions gives the best part of his life to the study of the Palmerston Papers at Broadlands and the archives of half a dozen capitals, no definitive life can be written until many have slaved at the galleys for many years.' Primarily this is because of the extraordinary length of time Palmerston spent in office—forty-eight years—a record that no British politician has come near to breaking. It is not surprising that a public life of this length should have furnished the material for very differing judgements; no man's record over such a period could be unmixed and it would be unlikely to be consistent.

Much has been written on Palmerston, yet rather less than might be expected; perhaps his political longevity has deterred potential authors. Soon after his death the prevailing tone of opinion became unenthusiastic and even hostile. Undoubtedly this was partly the result of the length of his career, for he seemed by the end to have outlasted his own times and thus the usual process of dating operated more swiftly than is customary. More important, however, were the influential enemies Palmerston had made; Talleyrand, his niece the Duchess of Dino and Princess Lieven used their considerable powers of persuasion against him, while the diarist Greville was for the most part hostile.

Also with time the feeling grew that Palmerston's style had been insupportable. A more apologetic Britain became ashamed of the national confidence and assertiveness that he had expressed. This attitude became strongest after the First World War, when Palmerston's forceful actions were judged to be warmongering. An essay of Harold Nicolson's in *The Great Victorians* demonstrates the depths to which his reputation had sunk when such an essentially fair-minded man, who had himself been a diplomat, could write: 'As Foreign Secretary he exposed his country to incessant alarums, driving the chariot of Britannia along the very brink of disaster.' Later in the same essay Nicolson claimed that Palmerston, 'in his endeavour to shine as the "Old English gentleman", became, as the years passed, more and more English and less and less of a gentleman; to him "self-preservation" became arrogance abroad'. Even H. F. C. Bell, writing a sympathetic biography between the Wars, constantly feels the need to apologise for his subject.

Increasing research, however, notably that of Sir Charles Webster, has painted another picture. Beneath Palmerston the intemperate has emerged Palmerston the cautious and wise. Much of the previously accepted canon has been shown to be based on prejudice and hostile witness. Certainly Palmerston is revealed by Webster's study of his first ten years at the Foreign Office as an extremely shrewd and skilful statesman. Southgate, in a recent book on Palmerston, has maintained the progress of his reputation. The faults of manner, the arrogance, the insensitivity, the egotism, remain; 'he devoted too much time to abuse and complaint of his opponents', wrote Webster. But they no longer prevent a balanced judgement of the man and his foreign policy. Just as some people are amused and attracted by his style, however, others are repelled, and a final valuation is not possible.

It is not surprising that one who was in the public's eye as long as Palmerston should be the subject of numerous anecdotes and the source of several legends. For some time in his middle years Palmerston was known as "Lord Cupid". It is claimed that the name originated with *The Times*, but whatever its source it drew attention to Palmerston the womaniser in a pejorative fashion, and its long currency testified to the wide acceptance of this view. He was generally recognised as the lover of Lady Cowper (the married sister of Lord Melbourne) long before she became his wife, he openly flaunted his many conquests, he was supposed to have attempted to rape one of the Queen's Ladies-in-Waiting at Windsor and at eighty-eight was cited as co-respondent in an abandoned divorce case. The nickname, however, also implies something of the drone; a quality even more implicit in the legend of "Pam" the "Regency Buck". Lord David Cecil in his *Lord M.* described Palmerston as a 'vulgar version of the Regency type, marked . . . by its characteristic blemishes of arrogance and insensitiveness'. His antecedents, his passionate interest in prize-fighting and horse-racing, his demeanour, his dress, his lack of intellectualism and his humour all mark him as the 'swell'. In fact Philip Guedalla went so far as to describe Palmerston as the 'last fragment of the eighteenth century'. This was the Palmerston who fought the architect's plans for a Gothic building for the new Foreign Office as a style 'swayed by erroneous views in religion and taste'; and who was described after a first meeting as having the 'air . . . more that of a man of the drawing-room than of the Senate'. It was the Palmerston who, speaking as Home Secretary on the licensing law, could joke that 'the words "licensed to be drunk on the Premises" are by the common People interpreted as applicable to the Customers as well as to the Liquor, and well do they avail themselves of the License'. It is easy to see why W. L. Burn rejected *The Age of Palmerston* as the title for his book in favour of *The Age of Equipoise*. 'What disqualified him', Burn writes of Palmerston, 'is his lack of the sober, serious, conscious thoughtfulness so characteristic of the age he lived into.'

Yet it would be as well to remember that there also exists the legend of Palmerston as the man who understood nineteenth-century England and in particular its middle class—Palmerston the archetypal John Bull. This was the Palmerston who was enormously popular in the country at large, who had long advocated freeing trade and who pressed for Limited Liability because it would release 'a great quantity of small capital' which might greatly benefit the country as well as its possessors. 'He knows the ignorance and the foibles of the people, and suits himself to them', argued his opponent Bright. 'He has never been deaf to the teachings of experience', claimed another writer; certainly it is difficult to portray Palmerston as ossified in a pre-1820 state of mind.

Another Palmerston legend is also summed up in a name he was given, "Lord Pumicestone". Bell wrote of 'his roughness, expressing itself more especially in an intolerable arrogance, and sometimes in an apparent desire to wound'. Palmerston was rude to the elderly and the distinguished just as much as to the young and the unknown. His rebukes and his hectoring lectures to fellow diplomats and subordinates are well known. The British Minister to Greece once received a 'specimen of the large round office hand for his sedulous imitation', together with a hint that 'ink ought to be black'. Nevertheless Palmerston always stood by those who served him faithfully whatever reproaches they might have had to bear from him. Lord Clarendon wrote to him once, 'I know by long experience that your support may always be relied upon by the agent or the colleague who does his best under difficult circumstances.' At the same time, however much Palmerston might offend by being brusque, he never harboured grudges, and had, asserted Gladstone, 'a nature incapable of enduring anger or the sentiment of wrath'.

Magnanimous, a bully, rakish and flippant he was, but, argues Webster, 'the final impression is one of immense energy, power of concentration, courage and resilience'. Palmerston's physical toughness is widely known; the enormous stamina that enabled him when Prime Minister to sit down and write reports on Parliamentary debates for the Queen at 4 a.m., and the fact that, in Bell's words, 'he could still (at seventy-five) take out a shooting party of young men, bring home a larger bag than any one of them, and beat them all at billiards after dinner'. Perhaps less generally recognised, however, is his incredible industry. For instance, the *Civis Romanus* speech of 1850 which won Palmerston so much popularity should perhaps be best known as an example of his powers of work. It described his foreign policy since 1830 at enormous length—it lasted over four-and-a-half hours—and was based on formidable research among the records. Southgate asserts that 'no man in public office ever worked harder or more conscientiously for so long'. Palmerston was no drone. Furthermore, though not a fluent parliamentary speaker, he was enormously competent professionally as a Foreign Secretary. He was at home in several languages, he was a tenacious negotiator, he was a skilled drafter of despatches and had a sure grasp of detail.

The tremendous demands that he made upon himself—and upon his subordinates—were still not enough to deal with the growing pressure of business. Webster believes that this was the root of Palmerston's chronic lack of punctuality. He was several times late both as host and guest of the Queen, but the best story of his failure to be aware of time is of the diner who arrived at Palmerston's house in Picaddilly to see his host departing on a before-dinner ride in Rotten Row. Certainly Palmerston's was a character to invite legends.

2 **The man and the career** The length of Viscount Palmerston's official career was not its only peculiarity; his late emergence as a front-rank political figure and the inordinately long time he spent in the one rather humble office of Secretary at War—eighteen years—both arouse speculation. Born in 1784, Henry John Temple was of Anglo-Irish stock, but for most of the past century, although relying for a large part of its income on estates in Ireland, his family had been established in England. His education at Harrow and Cambridge was conventional but was interrupted by a spell at the University of Edinburgh, at the time intellectually more stimulating than Cambridge. With his father's death in 1803 and his succession to an Irish peerage Palmerston was fortunate enough to have for his guardian the distinguished diplomat Lord Malmesbury. It was Malmesbury who obtained for him in 1807 a Junior Lordship of the Admiralty —the young man with estates mortgaged was in need of additional income—and he entered Parliament the same year.

In 1809 he was offered and refused the Chancellorship of the Exchequer by the new Prime Minister, Spencer Perceval. Not such an important post as it was to become, it was still a surprising offer to an inexperienced man, and Palmerston seems to have been somewhat scornful of a government in which he should have been proffered such a position. He also seems to have disliked the prospect of too burdensome an office, the same sentiment together with his love of London society persuading him later to decline the Chief Secretaryship of Ireland. Instead Palmerston became Secretary at War, a mainly administrative position not to be confused with the much more important Secretary of State for War and the Colonies. In this post Palmerston was extremely conscientious, 'an industrious plodder', but he was not prominent in Parliament and rarely spoke off his subject.

The great change in Palmerston's official life came in 1827 with Lord Liverpool's death and the succession of Canning. For, bereft of the support of the Ultra-Tories under the Duke of Wellington, Canning was more dependent upon the liberal Tories, of whom, as a believer in Catholic Emancipation and the freeing of trade, Palmerston was one. A scheme to make him Chancellor of the Exchequer was abandoned in the face of royal hostility and Palmerston resumed his old position, but now with a seat in the Cabinet. Webster writes of this development: 'It brought him access to Cabinet papers which transformed his whole outlook . . . Henceforth his main preoccupation was foreign affairs and the Foreign Office itself was'his goal'. It also gave him contact with the Landsdowne Whigs who served in Canning's Cabinet.

When the Duke of Wellington returned as Prime Minister, Palmerston, like the other "Canningites", felt unable to continue in government. It was in opposition that he first became a figure of consequence in Parliament when he delivered two bitter attacks on the foreign policy of the Duke's government. Greville wrote: 'This is the second [speech] he has made this year of great merit. It was very violent against Government . . . He has launched forth, and with astonishing success.' With the fall of the Duke, Grey and the Whigs came into office, and anxious for support and ministerial experience they turned to the Canning-ites. The obvious Whig candidates wishing for less onerous positions, Palmerston was offered and accepted the Foreign Secretaryship.

The circumstances of Palmerston's climb to the Foreign Office are important, for he was never really accepted by the Whigs as other than an expedient, and at any time in his career was believed capable of rejoining the Tories. When Melbourne, Grey's successor, returned to office in 1835 there was an unsuccessful attempt to remove Palmerston from the Foreign Office, which was repeated when Russell formed his Whig government in 1846. The Whigs were to remain jealous of a man they did not regard as one of themselves and hostile to his policy. Palmerston, however, was to remain necessary as the man who could help them maintain power. Outside Parliament his popularity made him an electoral asset, and inside Parliament he was supported by Radicals as the enemy of European reaction and by Tories as a British patriot. Finally, he was more acceptable to the "Peelites" than the true Whig Russell and he was able to secure their support in coalition. For with the break-up of the Conservatives over Peel's repeal of the Corn Laws the party was unable to form a viable government again in Palmerston's lifetime. This produced the situation of shifting forces and alliances in which a man of Palmerston's stature and determination could make himself indispensable, 'a Triton among the minnows'. Southgate in his *Passing of the Whigs* writes: 'The ill-considered Tory hack, rising by unorthodox methods, in association with the Whigs but not by the will of Whiggery, relying not on the connection but on himself, had reached a sort of Caesarian supremacy, making the Whigs dependent on him rather than he on them.' In 1852 he became Home Secretary in Aberdeen's coalition and succeeded him as Prime Minister in 1855, an office he was to hold until his death in 1865 save for one break of sixteen months from 1858 to 1859.

It is impossible to discuss the career of Palmerston without treating of his relations with Queen Victoria. Difficulty between minister and Sovereign developed during Palmerston's third term as Foreign Secretary after 1846, and reached the point where she pressed the Prime Minister, Russell, for his dismissal. Although Victoria was later to have Palmerston as her Prime Minister for nine years she continued to distrust him, particularly in his foreign policy. Disagreement at first arose over the generally pro-constitutionalist line that Palmerston took in relation to affairs in Europe, but it was greatly magnified during the revolutions of 1848. Victoria and Albert, 'very conscious of their membership of the European union of princes', were horrified at Palmerston's apparent desire to see Austria forced out of Italy.

The quarrel, however, increasingly widened into one of constitutional principle. The Queen and her husband corresponded privately with members of their family—particularly King Leopold of Belgium and the Prince Consort of Portugal—a correspondence Palmerston did not see and suspected of opposing his policy. Meanwhile Victoria sought to exploit her constitutional right to know what was being done in her name to tone down Palmerston's despatches. As a result Palmerston became more devious and sent off despatches without first showing drafts to the Queen, or else altered them after they had been approved. Lord Russell, the Prime Minister, was drawn into the dispute, especially as Palmerston was sometimes equally neglectful of informing the Cabinet about his actions. The outcome was that Palmerston accepted the Queen's memorandum demanding that she be informed in advance by the Foreign Secretary on his course of action.

Nevertheless relations were further exacerbated by various incidents. Palmerston's strictures on Austria's reactionary policy were answered by no Habsburg archduke being sent to London to intimate the accession to the Austrian throne of Francis Joseph. An Austrian general, Haynau, on a visit to a London brewery was manhandled by draymen incensed at his cruelty in suppressing the Hungarian revolt, and Palmerston was only lukewarm in his regrets. Then in 1851 Kossuth, the exiled Hungarian leader, visited England. Palmerston, most reluctantly dissuaded from receiving him personally, nevertheless accepted a deputation of London Radicals with an address that referred to the Austrian Emperor and the Tsar as 'odious and detestable assassins', the words of Kossuth. As well as the Queen it seemed that Russell had now had enough and he wrote to Palmerston to this effect.

In all these incidents, however, he had the support of the country and so Russell could do little. Never was this truer than in Palmerston's defence of actions over the seizure of Greek shipping to enforce payment of compensation by the Greek Government to Don Pacifico. In his greatest speech, *Civis Romanus Sum*, he proclaimed his determination that Englishmen's rights should be protected throughout the world, and received rapturous popular support. At the end of 1851, however, Palmerston conveyed his private pleasure at the success of Louis Napoleon's successful *coup d'état* against the French Assembly. This seemingly anti-constitutional attitude was not popular, and Russell used Palmerston's action, which had not been in accord with Cabinet policy, to force his dismissal. In the subsequent debate Russell introduced the Royal Memorandum as a further way of discrediting Palmerston. For the time being it seemed that the Queen had succeeded in freeing herself from the Minister she so disliked. 'There was a Palmerston', opined Disraeli. In fact, within two months of his own dismissal, Palmerston was to reassert himself by leading the House in the overthrow of the Russell Government.

Russell and Palmerston had been rivals and colleagues since 1830, and Russell was only to outlast Palmerston by one year in public life although he lived for a further decade. Their careers were entwined, for just as Palmerston had been Russell's Foreign Secretary from 1846–51 so Russell was to be Palmerston's from 1859–65. Russell was surprisingly docile under Palmerston, partly because of his inexperience in foreign affairs, partly because the two agreed on such issues as the Polish revolt and Italian unity. Seaman wrote that Russell's 'views on foreign policy were those of a Whig idealist, hating Tsars as passionately as he hated Popes'; and it does seem that Palmerston was the more restrained of the two. A Cabinet colleague claimed that Palmerston 'in every important case suggests to Lord John what to do. Lord John brings it before the Cabinet as his own idea, and then Palmerston supports him, as if the case was new to him.' In fact Palmerston appears to have guided British foreign policy until his death.

3 Whose disciple? 'The small political party to which I belonged while out of office . . . was the instrument in placing me in the office which I now hold', was Palmerston's comment in a letter of 1832; the office was that of Foreign Secretary, the small party was that of the Canningites. It is not surprising that Palmerston has been, in the inevitable comparisons with his great predecessors Castlereagh and Canning, most often seen as a disciple of Canning. The speeches on foreign affairs which first brought him prominence in 1829 were indictments of the Tory Government for failing to pursue the policies of Canning over Portugal, and his own policies in Spain and Portugal were designed to rectify the mistake. In speeches and despatches he attacked the continental 'tyrants' and developed further the role of Canning as the scourge of Metternich. Similarly his forthright statements of British interest and his courting of popular support were the ways of Canning. He asserted in 1848 that he 'would adopt the expression of Canning and say that with every British Minister the interests of England ought to be the Shibboleth of his policy'. Professor Bell appears to have much on his side when he writes: 'In his [Palmerston's] desire that England should stand upon her own feet, his appreciation of the great force of public sentiment, and his taste for constitutional government as the proper medium between autocracy and democracy, he was a natural-born Canningite.' Some writers have gone further and seen Palmerston as distorting Canning's policies by following them beyond their author's intentions. Algernon Cecil believed that Palmerston's policy 'very well exemplified the nemesis of the system of Canning. Starting with the principle of every nation for itself, he was perpetually confronted with the fact that no nation is, or can be, purely self-regarding.' In this picture Palmerston is portrayed as the antithesis of Castlereagh, who had believed that

Britain should always work through Europe. But is this picture an accurate one?

It is perhaps significant that it was a former student of Castlereagh, Sir Charles Webster, who found as he turned his attention to Palmerston that the popular image of Palmerston as the disciple of Canning was unsatisfactory. Webster in fact came to the conclusion that 'his attitude towards Europe . . . was indeed more that of Castlereagh than of Canning'. The basis for this assertion is that Palmerston, in the words of Seaman, 'saw that the path to peace was the path of negotiation, undertaken in collaboration with the other powers'. In the great crises of his Foreign Secretaryship Palmerston realised that European solutions were necessary. Thus with the Belgian revolt he knew that the only satisfactory outcome was one arrived at by agreement of the Powers, and he employed a conference of ambassadors of the major Powers to achieve it. Likewise he came to discern that the Eastern Question could only be satisfactorily dealt with in a European context. Hence the crisis created by Mehemet Ali's threat to the Ottoman Sultan saw Palmerston seeking to build a European Concert, even though this meant acting with Russia and Austria, whose reactionary policies he personally abhorred. Where Canning had seemed to delight in seeing the consensus of the Powers shattered over the Eastern Question at the time of the Greek revolt, Palmerston worked to restore it from 1839–41. As with the Belgian revolt he neither asked for nor wished any territorial prize for Britain; European stability was enough. His policy was to prevent any Power, Russia in the early 1830s and at the time of the Crimean War, or France in 1839–41, from seeking to impose a unilateral settlement. Any change must come through general agreement, and Britain should be prepared to threaten war on any state that tried to dictate its own solutions.

The events of 1848–9 further demonstrated Palmerston's understanding that Britain's interests demanded calm and peace in Europe. Thus the temptation to gloat at the casting down of tyranny must be resisted. Amid the chaos of revolution Britain and Russia were, as Palmerston announced, 'the only two Powers in Europe that remain standing upright, and we ought to look with confidence to each other'. Despite the popularity of the Hungarian cause in England, he made no ringing denunciation of Russian action in assisting Austria to suppress the Hungarian revolt. 'Palmerston', as Webster claims, 'like Castlereagh was well aware of the complexity of European problems, [and] the interest of Britain in them all.' Even with the Polish revolts against the Tsar in 1831 and 1863 Palmerston showed his awareness of the European situation as a whole. In 1831, although privately pleading for clemency for the Poles, he was at pains to avoid embarrassing the Tsar with public complaint, and in 1863, despite the worries of Queen Victoria, there was no chance that he would go to war to resurrect Poland.

Nevertheless, as Webster has suggested, 'to Castlereagh's conception of a Concert of the Great Powers he added that protection of Liberalism which Canning had threatened but never carried out'. Most certainly the 'protection of Liberalism' cannot be discovered in Castlereagh's policies, but what about Canning? Southgate suggests that Canning might well have intervened in Portugal, as did Palmerston, to restore Queen Maria, but 'more probably he would have worked to restore Maria *without* the Charter [the Constitution], which he did not think suitable for Portugal'. In fact Southgate asserts that 'Palmerston . . . was deceived by Canning's propaganda into believing that Canning had been a Palmerstonian.'

'The system of England', affirmed Palmerston, 'ought to be to maintain the liberties and independence of all other nations . . . to throw her moral weight into the scale of any people who are spontaneously striving for freedom, by which I mean rational government, and to extend as far and as fast as possible civilisation all over the world.' He believed that this policy—obviously it would conflict at times with his concern for the Concert of Powers —should be pursued as far as possible short of war. Intervention on this scale had never been part of Canning's policies, indeed he claimed to have extracted Britain from Europe in cases where her interests were not vitally concerned.

There was one aspect of Palmerston's work, however, where he may justifiably be declared the follower of Canning—the manner in which he strove to enlist popular support for his policies. Like Canning, Palmerston was never a true party man and lacked real parliamentary backing; he therefore turned to the country. The way in which Palmerston tried to mould public opinion was twofold. First he published an unprecedented quantity of information for Parliament. Webster's judgement is that 'the total amount of information given to Parliament on all the diplomacy . . . was impressive, and it did a great deal to enlighten public opinion all over Europe'. Even more significant, however, was Palmerston's use of the Press.

It had become fairly clear by this time that the British Press could not be bought, but Palmerston recognised the influence that could be obtained by supplying newspapers with information. He described the technique: 'Every now and then when we have any particular piece of news, it is given to the editor and he thereby gets a start of his competitors, and on condition of receiving the occasional intimation he gives his support to the Government.' Palmerston also wrote regularly but anonymously for *The Globe*. He chose an evening paper because he found it a convenient way to reply to criticism in the morning papers, particularly *The Times* after he had fallen foul of it in 1834. An interesting example of Palmerston's awareness of the Press is the manner in which he timed election speeches in his constituency at Tiverton so that reporters could catch the train for London in time for the first editions; a curious precedent for the current timing of government announcements to receive maximum television coverage.

Although in this respect Palmerston was similar to Canning, it is impossible to make out a convincing case for his being the latter's disciple. Perhaps the final judgement must be that Palmerston was too independent and original a man to have been the disciple of Castlereagh, Canning or anybody else.

4 Progressive or patriot? 'In terms of man-hours', claims Southgate, 'the suppression of the slave trade was the principal occupation of the Foreign Office under Palmerston.' A naval squadron was kept off the West African coast and treaties were signed with France in 1831–3 and Spain in 1835 which gave mutual rights of search of suspected slave ships. Because Portugal unofficially connived at the traffic, Palmerston gained parliamentary approval in 1839 'to do ourselves and on our own authority that which Portugal herself refuses to permit us to do by Treaty'. Brazil was likewise coerced, and the slave trade was only carried on in ships from the United States, until at the time of the Civil War that too was stopped with the Treaty of 1862 between Britain and the United States.

Palmerston was attacked in Parliament by the Cobdenites for the wanton extravagance of his policies and encountered little enthusiasm for the job from the Royal Navy; the success of his policy depended to a large extent on his own determination. It might seem that his motives must go unquestioned, but some historians have pointed out that slavery allowed foreign sugar plantations an advantage in labour costs over the plantations with emancipated workers in the British West Indies. Palmerston, however, in his own writings gives the lie to this interpretation of his actions; he believed that free trade and competition would demonstrate the greater productivity of paid labour. He saw the suppression of the slave trade as 'the achievement which I look back to with the greatest and the purest pleasure'.

Palmerston's reputation as a progressive does not, of course, rest only upon his work against the traffic in slaves. Throughout Europe he appeared to thwart the policies of Metternich and European reaction. Thus he succeeded in delaying action by the Powers over Switzerland in 1847, when a split in the Federation had occurred, until the minority group of conservative Cantons, the Sonderbund, had been crushed by the more liberal majority. Although only a late convert to the principles of the Reform Bill, Palmerston was a sincere advocate of constitutional government. In a private letter he clearly stated his general attachment to the principle: 'You say that a constitution is but a means to an end and the end is good government: but the experience of mankind shews that this is the only road by which the goal can be reached and that it is impossible without a constitution fully to develop the natural resources of a country and to ensure for the nation security for life, liberty and property.'

All over Europe Palmerston pressed for the granting of constitutions, as in Italy where, in the Papal States in particular, he believed that the introduction of some form of representative system was the only way of alleviating dreadful misrule. Again, in Greece, he used all Britain's influence as one of the protecting Powers to press for a 'real and *bona fide* Constitution . . . in order that the measures of the Government should be calculated to promote the general welfare'. It was, however, in the Iberian peninsula that Palmerston's most determined and consistent attempts to establish constitutional rule were made.

Both Spain and Portugal were, in the 1830s, to be the scene of struggles for succession between girl heirs to the throne and their uncles. The two struggles became related because the participants correctly recognised that the outcome in one would considerably affect the result in the other. In both cases the young Queens were identified, albeit falsely, with constitutional rule, and their uncles, Dom Miguel in Portugal and Don Carlos in Spain, with reaction and clericalism, and other European states favoured one side or the other according to their political views. For his part Palmerston had no doubt: 'It is there . . . that is to be decided by issue of battle that great contest between opposing and conflicting principles of government—arbitrary government on the one hand and constitutional government on the other—which is going on all over Europe.' He was certain that Britain must try to ensure that the young Queens triumphed, and it was over Wellington's failure to assist Maria in Portugal that Palmerston had spoken so indignantly to Parliament in 1829.

The causes of the two Queens were pressed by parents: in Portugal the father of Maria, Dom Pedro, who had waived his claim to the Portuguese throne, and in Spain, Isabella's mother Christina, after 1833 the widowed Queen Regent. Their level of ability and purity of motive, however, as with the other protagonists was extraordinarily low, and in the case of Queen Christina lust was added to financial greed and rapacity. In the opinion of the British ambassador, Christina quarrelled with one Chief Minister because he declined her advances, and was engaged in building up her wealth outside the country. In Portugal after Miguel's defeat in 1834, and subsequently in Spain as Don Carlos became a nuisance rather than a threat, Britain found herself increasingly caught up in the rivalries between parties of constitutionalists. In Portugal Britain sided with the more moderate *Chartists* against the *Septembrists*, but in Spain she favoured the more democratic *Progressistas* in opposition to the *Moderados*.

When Palmerston became Foreign Secretary in 1830 the cause of Maria in Portugal was at a very low ebb, while in Spain it seemed that King Ferdinand might accept his brother rather than his daughter as heir. In Britain, and even in the Cabinet, Palmerston encountered antagonism to a policy which would involve the country in Iberian affairs and necessitate expense. At the same time he had to face opposition from France, who was jealous of British influence in Portugal and ambitious for her own position in Spain. In short it was a most unpromising situation, and it was hardly surprising that Aberdeen had chosen to withdraw British troops from Portugal and reduce involvement in the area. Palmerston, however, had no intention of following him. 'Why, . . . do what we will, there is a fatality which draws us like the moth into the candle, to entangle ourselves in the internal affairs of Portugal', Palmerston claimed; later he asserted it to be an 'English interest that the cause of the Queen of Spain shall be successful'.

In pursuit of this policy Palmerston was able to give some direct assistance with marines and the navy, but largely he was forced to employ indirect means. Thus he was behind the creation of the British Legion for Spain, an international force of over 8,000 men mainly officered by retired British officers and commanded by a Radical M.P. He agreed to the fitting out in Britain of a naval expedition of Dom Pedro's and allowed English half-pay naval officers to serve in it. Charles Napier, who subsequently commanded this force under the name of Carlo Ponza, with his dash and energy was instrumental in the improvement of Dom Pedro's and his daughter's position. Above all Palmerston involved himself with intrigue and advice in Portuguese and Spanish affairs; to gain military victory, to abate the cruelty of his protégés, to protect the constitutions and to find a husband for Maria of Portugal. In his efforts he was greatly assisted after 1823 by the British ambassador at Madrid, George Villiers, later as Earl of Clarendon himself Foreign Secretary.

Palmerston realised the necessity for an alliance between the Queens of Spain and Portugal but was hampered by Portuguese distrust of Spanish motive. It was to reduce this suspicion and to ensure British naval assistance that in 1834 Britain allied herself with Spain and Portugal. The alliance was then, as the Quadruple Alliance, extended to include France; although the French would have preferred a full military alliance with Britain this remained, in Southgate's words, 'essentially a device for the settlement of affairs in the Peninsula according to British prescriptions'. In Portugal it was completely successful, leading to Dom Miguel's immediate defeat, but it was also very important in Spain.

The alliance, both at the time and since, has been judged by some people to mark a decisive stage in European affairs, as ranging the constitutional states against the autocracies. Palmerston himself wrote: 'It establishes a quadruple alliance among the constitutional states of the West, which will serve as a powerful counterpoise to the Holy Alliance of the East.' This interpretation, however, is hardly borne out by subsequent Anglo-French rivalries in the Peninsula, to say nothing of the more serious split over the Near East. Certainly it suited Palmerston to allow the alliance to be seen as a riposte to the agreements just concluded by the Eastern Courts following upon their meeting at München-grätz, and certainly the drafting and signing of the Treaty was a considerable triumph for Palmerston's skill—'a capital hit and all my own doing', he claimed. He also asserted that 'the Spaniards and Portuguese . . . with the consent of their legitimate sovereigns, and with the protecting aid of England, have obtained for themselves the inestimable blessing of representative government'. The subsequent history of the nineteenth century hardly bears this out, even if it is difficult to accept Pemberton's conclusion that 'of all the measures associated with his name, those which he took in connexion with Spain were the most lacking in lustre and significance'.

In certain situations Palmerston advocated the granting of a constitution or the liberalising of a government as necessary to prevent a revolution which he believed to be damaging to British interests, a policy which would, he argued, 'separate by reasonable concessions the moderate from the exaggerated, content the former . . . and get them to assist in resisting the insatiable demands of the latter'. For the 'exaggerated' and 'insatiable demands' he had no sympathy. The same sort of calculation lay behind Palmerston's attitudes to the hopes of national unification and independence cherished by so many Europeans in the mid-nineteenth century. Italy is of particular interest, for it was here that Palmerston advocated both concession to nationalist aspirations and the granting of constitutions as the means of obviating far more serious and fundamental change. Palmerston feared Italy as a potential source of danger, not only because he believed that the refusal of legitimate demands would eventually lead to a great explosion, but also because of its strategic position. Italy, so often in the past the first objective of an aggressive France, was after 1815 dominated by Austria. For this reason Italian grievance and French aggression, disguised as altruistic aid to a tyrannised people, might easily combine to bring about a European war.

The Italian problem thrust itself to the forefront on three occasions during Palmerston's period of office. The least serious was in 1831, when revolutions which had broken out in various parts of Italy were suppressed by Austrian arms. The second was in 1848–9, when revolution spread throughout Italy and became merged with a war waged by Sardinia-Piedmont against Austria with the objective of delivering the peninsula from Habsburg influence. The Pope was driven from his lands and republics were set up, but finally Austria emerged victorious; this at a time when revolution in France had instituted in the Second Republic a regime which could only see the Vienna settlement of 1815 as a defeat. Finally in 1859, Napoleon III's war with Austria as the ally of Sardinia-Piedmont created a situation of flux in which the Italian state was finally created.

The two closely interwoven strands of Palmerston's Italian policy were the attempt to secure constitutions and amelioration of conditions in the Italian states, and the endeavour to prevent France from acting unilaterally in Italy. At first his main consideration was, in Webster's words, 'to remove some of the worst evils under which the Italian people suffered'. This was the motive of Palmerston's decision that the Earl of Minto, a Cabinet colleague, should in 1847 go to Italy to press for reform. Southgate writes that this mission was 'dictated by a belief that Austrian policy was driving Italy, and Europe, to revolution and war, and that both could be avoided only by the grant of constitutions'. Palmerston had come to believe that the proper solution was the extrusion of Austria from the peninsula, because Italy had become to Austria 'the heel of Achilles, and not the shield of Ajax'.

Thus during 1848–9 he strove to mediate between Sardinia-Piedmont and Austria. 'It was obvious to him', asserts Southgate, 'that he must not only seek to localise the war, by keeping the French out, but to end it as soon as possible, because the longer it went on, the more likely the French were to intervene.' He believed that this meant achieving autonomy for Lombardy and Venetia, although perhaps retaining some Austrian connection. He stated his aim at the time: 'I should wish to see the whole of Northern Italy united in one kingdom . . . Such an arrangement . . . would be most conducive to the peace of Europe, by interposing between France and Austria a neutral state strong enough to make itself respected.' At the same time Palmerston sought to limit the action of France, if necessary by joining with her and harnessing her energy by proposals of joint mediation, 'the only step which could keep a French army out of Italy and so avert a general war', claims A. J. P. Taylor. As the tide turned and Austria triumphed Palmerston did all he could short of war to secure acceptable terms for Piedmont.

Believing, as he did, that 'the Austrians have no business in Italy, and they are a public nuisance there', it is not surprising that when he returned as Prime Minister in 1859, Palmerston had no intention of doing anything to maintain Austria against Napoleon III's attempt to throw her out of Italy. In the period of uncertainty which followed the truce of Villafranca Palmerston welcomed efforts by the Central Italian states to combine with Piedmont, although the Cabinet would not allow him to give any official encouragement. He was deeply offended by France's annexation of Savoy and Nice as the price of her acceptance of Piedmont's expansion in Central Italy and continued to distrust Napoleon III thereafter. He refused to join in any armed mediation to prevent Garibaldi's landing in Sicily or crossing to Naples, and along with Russell he applauded the results of the amazing expedition which created a united Italy.

Despite his benevolence towards Italian unification and his early enthusiasm for Greek independence, Palmerston was no believer in nationalism—that central cause of nineteenth-century progressives. Disraeli accused Palmerston of being a convert to the 'sentimental principle of nationality', but this is impossible to substantiate; 'the policy of Palmerston was not based upon sentimental considerations of nationalism but upon the enduring principles of the Balance of Power', asserts A. J. P. Taylor. His disinterest in German unification and his positive hostility to Serbian and Romanian nationalism are incontrovertible, and his sympathy for Poland never extended to doing anything which might lead to war with Russia. Above all Palmerston's refusal in 1849 even to declare in speeches against the suppression of the Hungarian revolt was unpopular with many of his supporters as well as contrary to the principle of nationalism.

In the same way his opposition to Austrian policies was not, as so many believed, part of a general progressive hostility to the Austrian Empire. He talked of the Empire as 'a thing worth saving'. Southgate averred that 'Palmerston aspired to be the surgeon, not the murderer, of the Habsburg Empire'. The description of Palmerston, then, as a progressive cannot be accepted without serious reservations. It has been argued, in fact, that his progressive policies were concerned to serve the interests of Britain rather than those of constitutionalism or progress. Thus one French historian, Barante, believed that Palmerston patronised constitutionalism to weaken the main rivals of Britain on the Continent.

With his reference to British prestige and influence, his embracing of patriotic causes, his preoccupation with strengthening Britain's defences, it sometimes seems that Palmerston's policies were those of a British nationalist. He claimed: 'I have . . . endeavoured to maintain the Dignity and to uphold the Interests of the Country abroad.' It was this sort of statement that led Gavin Henderson to write that if Palmerston had a theme 'it was a narrow and bigoted desire to enhance Britain's prestige'. But this will not do. Perhaps Algernon Cecil is nearer the truth when he suggests that Palmerston had two aims—the general advancement of right and justice and the particular advancement of British interests. 'Happily for his peace of mind', Cecil writes, 'these objects never seemed to him to disagree.'

5 Blusterer or statesman?　Bell, the biographer of Palmerston, talks of his subject's 'meddlesomeness, obstinacy, touches of bombast and hauteur, the tendency to create enmities and invite slights'. Sometimes this picture is allowed to predominate in writers' views of Palmerston to the extent of ignoring his finesse or nicety of timing. Instead he emerges as one who could not manage personal relationships, who because of his brusquerie and rudeness alienated old friends and failed to capitalise on the strong position of his country. With states that were weak it is said Palmerston was able to get away with his failings, but when he came to deal with the more powerful or less easily bluffed his ineptitude was exposed. The Don Pacifico incident serves as an example of how Palmerston could win a cheap and useless triumph over a feeble Greek state; the attempt to appoint Stratford Canning as ambassador to St. Petersburg, the affair of the Spanish marriages, and particularly the crisis over Schleswig-Holstein are examples of his failures.

The circumstances of Stratford Canning's appointment are fairly straightforward, if judgements of Palmerston's handling of it are not. From 1830 it was clear there would soon have to be a new ambassador at St. Petersburg. As early as 1831 Princess

Lieven, the wife of the Russian ambassador in London, had warned that it might be Stratford Canning (cousin of George Canning and later Viscount Stratford de Redcliffe). Despite immediate opposition from Russia Palmerston made the appointment in 1832. The Tsar refused to accept Canning, Palmerston declined to back down, and as Britain had no ambassador in Russia the Tsar recalled Lieven in 1833. Talleyrand believed the whole episode to be the product of Palmerston's determination to get rid of Princess Lieven; others have seen it as a stubborn refusal to subordinate personal pride to national benefit. Certainly Palmerston was angered by Princess Lieven's intrigue behind his back. Webster, however, argues that Canning's claims to the post were strong and that Palmerston's behaviour was reasonable. Whatever its other effects, it has to be admitted that the incident rendered British relations with Russia more difficult.

The affair of the Spanish Marriages, in Southgate's words 'the result of Palmerston's ineptitude', occurred after Palmerston's return to office in 1846. Aberdeen and Guizot, in the search for acceptable husbands for the Spanish Queen Isabella and her sister the Infanta Louisa, had agreed upon a Bourbon for the Queen, most probably one of her Spanish cousins, the Duke of Cadiz or the Duke of Seville. The former, however, was widely believed to be impotent and the latter, besides being personally repugnant, was odious to the Queen Mother as the patron of the progressives. For the younger sister Aberdeen had accepted a son of Louis Philippe, provided the Queen was already married and had produced an heir to the throne. Palmerston pushed too hard for the Duke of Seville, and incautiously allowed the French to copy a despatch in which he was bitingly critical of the Spanish government—a copy the French showed to the Spanish. In this way he irritated Spain to the point where Isabella was promptly married to the Duke of Cadiz whilst at the same time her sister married a son of Louis Philippe. This brought Louis Philippe no long-term benefit but was widely accepted as a diplomatic triumph. Palmerston was believed, even by Victoria, to have been cruelly used, but the incident was nevertheless seen as the fruit of his former hectoring and continued lack of caution and tact.

The failure which it is impossible to deny is Palmerston's part in the Prussian and Austrian seizure of Schleswig-Holstein in 1864. Twice the problem of Schleswig-Holstein faced Palmerston, first in 1848 when his policy seemed to secure a great triumph, and then again in 1863-4 when in somewhat humiliating circumstances he only narrowly escaped a vote of censure in the Commons. The basic problem was the same on both occasions. The Duchies, separate but long associated, were ruled by the King of Denmark. Holstein, entirely German, was a member of the German Confederation, but Schleswig, with a large Danish minority, was not. In Denmark, mounting nationalism demanded the incorporation of Schleswig, while in Germany public opinion insisted that the Duchies were inseparable, and it was urged that Schleswig become part of the Confederation.

A crisis was reached when it seemed that the Danish crown would pass through the female line, whereas it was argued that the Duchies could not and that the Duke of Augustenburg was the rightful heir. 1848 brought a revolt in the Duchies against Danish attempts to incorporate Schleswig which was supported by Prussian troops acting for the Frankfurt Parliament. Britain, France and Russia had all shown themselves hostile to German actions and Palmerston had striven for a reversion to the *status quo ante*. Although the treaty was not signed until 1852 Palmerston had secured the substance before he left office in 1851. Augustenburg's claim was bought out and Christian of Glucksburg recognised as heir to the Duchies as well as Denmark, which, however, were to remain separate.

In 1863, on Christian's accession, fresh steps were taken by the Danes towards incorporation while Augustenburg proclaimed the rights of his son and was supported militarily by the German Confederation. At this stage Prussia, with Bismarck as Prime Minister, persuaded Austria to join in occupation of Schleswig as a guarantee of Denmark's fulfilling her obligations. After imposing impossible demands, Prussia and Austria resumed fighting in 1864, and, after an abortive international conference, they dictated peace terms to the Danes and took the Duchies for themselves.

Opinion in Britain, with the important exception of the Queen, who believed in the legitimacy of German action, was shocked by the browbeating of a small state. At the same time there was strong dislike for a strategically important area passing to Germany. Nevertheless there was little public willingness to go to war on behalf of the Danes. The failure of Palmerston was that, in Southgate's words, 'he failed to deter the Germans but encouraged the Danes to be stubborn'. Despite continual protest and talk of sending the fleet to protect Copenhagen, Palmerston never intended that Britain should fight, and certainly the Cabinet would never have accepted war, but his warning that 'those who made the attempt [to overthrow Danish rights] would find in the result that it would not be Denmark alone with which they would have to contend' had not assisted the Danes to realise that they were on their own.

Some writers have seen Bismarck as too astute for Palmerston, others have stressed Palmerston's failure to understand German nationalism: 'To German nationalism as a force in European politics he still seemed blind', asserted Bell. More important, perhaps, was the failure of Palmerston to judge the changed European situation that rendered previously successful policies no longer applicable. Increasing distrust for France over Louis Napoleon III's Italian policy had been reflected in 1863 by Britain's failure to go beyond protest against Russia's subjection of the Poles. France had scorned this as pusillanimous, and when Britain came out against Napoleon's project of a Congress to consider European affairs, the Entente was shattered. Therefore Palmerston was not able to carry conviction in 1864 when he tried to threaten Prussia with French action in support of Denmark. At the same time Bismarck realised that Palmerston would in the last resort prefer German aggression against Denmark to French aggression on the Rhine; 'he knew it was foolish to invite a major shift in the Balance of Power to avoid a lesser one'.

Palmerston, however, was a very old man by this time, and it seems unfair to judge him too harshly because of this mistake; neither Canning nor Castlereagh lived into the period when their policies had ceased to be workable. Even so, Palmerston was adapting himself to the new situation before he died and was writing that 'Germany ought to be strong in order to resist Russian aggression, and a strong Prussia is essential to German strength'. Temperley and Penson judge that 'even humiliation cannot blind him to reality or prevent his view from being statesmanlike'.

There are many occasions that demonstrate the statesman and exhibit the very tact some critics of Palmerston deny him. Of particular interest is a letter to Stratford Canning in 1849. Palmerston, having successfully supported the Sultan in resisting demands for the extradition of refugees, including Kossuth, who sought sanctuary in Turkey after the crushing of the Hungarian revolt, wrote, 'But all this *we* ought not to boast of, and on the contrary we must let our baffled Emperors pass as quietly and as decently as possible over the bridge by which they are going to retreat.'

It is interesting that Palmerston's two major domestic defeats were both the result of his being too statesmanlike and disdaining opportunities for demagogic success. His dismissal from office in 1851 followed a forward-looking expression of personal satisfaction at Louis Napoleon's coup, and the fall of his government in 1858 was occasioned by his decision to act in response to foreign outcry. Finally, and in some ways most surprising, Palmerston's handling of the problems occasioned by the American Civil War demonstrates tact and awareness: 'The only thing to do seems to be to lie on our oars, and to give no pretext to the Washingtonians to quarrel with us.' Even when, in 1861, two Southern envoys were seized from the British Mail Steamer *Trent*, Palmerston refused to behave rashly. It is true that Prince Albert helped to secure moderation in this instance, but Palmerston, although demonstrating just how seriously he took the incident, realised the importance of allowing the Federal Government the opportunity to climb down gracefully. A hostile critic of the Palmerston government was forced to accept that over the Civil War it had displayed 'most prudent and commendable forbearance in spite of great temptations to the contrary'.

These examples alone demonstrate that Palmerston was much more than a mere blusterer, but to judge just how consummate his diplomacy could be and how statesmanlike his policies it is necessary to turn to two triumphs: the creation of Belgium and his handling of the Eastern Question after 1839. The creation of an independent Belgium is rightly seen as one of Palmerston's greatest triumphs and is particularly surprising in that it was the work of one inexperienced in the conduct of high diplomacy, especially when he was confronted by so many experienced professionals. It is this inexperience that has led some historians to claim that much of the credit should go to Grey. This view, however, along with the belief that Palmerston wished to destroy the commercial strength of Holland as a potential rival to Britain, must be abandoned in the light of recent research.

In 1830, inspired by the July Revolution in Paris, the Belgians revolted against their Dutch ruler. Finding himself hard pressed, King William appealed to the four Powers of the Quadruple Alliance, who had been behind the setting up of his state in 1814–15, to subdue the revolt. Wellington had no intention of trying to act in this way, realising that it would push France to war on behalf of the Belgians. Instead negotiations were begun in London at a conference of the ambassadors of the major Powers, including France, to find some way of reconciling the demands of the Belgians with those of the Dutch, the conference being chaired by the British Foreign Secretary. Thus when Palmerston became Foreign Secretary in November he 'inherited from Wellington both a policy and an instrument'.

Various deleterious possibilities faced Britain: Belgium might become a French client state, be annexed outright, be partitioned with France receiving a large share, or France might find herself driven into a European war on her behalf. Britain's need, now that one viable state seemed impossible, was two viable states— in Palmerston's words, 'to make Belgium independent and Holland prosperous and strong'. Palmerston saw this from the first and fought to secure it with determination and enormous energy—on occasion he got his way from the fatigue and hunger of his fellow negotiators—but also with guile and expertise.

Talleyrand wrote in his *Memoires*, on the strength of these negotiations, that Palmerston was one of the ablest men of affairs, if not the ablest, that he had encountered in his career.

The immediate principles Palmerston struggled to establish were that the United Netherlands be accepted as dissolved and that none of the major Powers should gain advantage from the dissolution. By the middle of January he had secured the former, and a Belgian delegation had been despatched to the Conference, where it was treated on a par with the Dutch. He had also secured a 'self-denying' Protocol from the Powers but failed to enlarge this into an agreement that no member of the ruling houses of the Powers should occupy the Belgian throne; the French and the Belgians were scheming to secure the throne for a son of Louis Philippe. The Eastern Powers, although disliking the acceptance of a state born in revolution, and deeply suspicious of Louis Philippe, were preoccupied with revolt in Poland and Italy; hence it was necessary for Palmerston to take the lead against French schemes. Fleet movements and forthright diplomatic warnings were enough to get the French to abandon their schemes and accept Leopold of Coburg as the Belgian King.

It was now the turn of the Dutch to object, and they launched an invasion of Belgium. The Eastern Powers, favouring the King of Holland, were unlikely to do anything, whereas France was certain to act to save the new Belgian state. Palmerston's achievement was to control French military action by presenting it as the upholding of decisions of the London Conference and employing the British fleet to add conviction to his interpretation. After a successful intervention the French showed some reluctance to withdraw from Belgium and again it was left to Palmerston to make France see she was Europe's and not her own agent in this matter. 'The French must go out of Belgium', he warned, 'or we have a general war, and war in a given number of days.' The essentials of the eventual agreement were accepted by November 1831 although the Dutch remained obdurate, and further military action followed by naval blockade by France and England was necessary before they agreed to accept Belgian independence. It was not until 1839 that the final agreement was made in the

Treaty of London, with Belgian neutrality guaranteed by the Powers.

Particular problems arose over the exact geographical frontiers, the rights of navigation on the Scheldt and the allocation of respective shares in the Netherlands national debt. In all these matters Palmerston exhibited enormous attention to detail and factual mastery of complicated subject-matter while persisting in his aim that both the states must be viable. Taking his stand on European interest Palmerston was able to ally with the Eastern Powers to check France, to work with France against the Dutch and their potential supporters, the Eastern Powers, and to deal with Belgium as one friend who had no aims of annexation or partition. In this way he secured a peaceful solution to a problem pregnant with dangers of war.

His handling of the Eastern Question exhibited the same aware-ness of the European nature of the problem, once he had realised the importance of the issue. Palmerston's initial incursion in Near Eastern affairs was the setting up of the Greek state under Otto of Bavaria and the definition of its frontiers in 1832. In his view of Near Eastern affairs at this time Palmerston was a sup-porter of the Greeks, he had no real fear of Russia, and had little idea about what was to be the critical issue in the area during the next decade—the struggle between the Sultan in Constantinople and his nominal vassal, the Pasha of Egypt. It is clear from his writings that Palmerston was not certain whether Britain's inter-ests would best be served by siding with Mahmud II or with Mehemet Ali.

Hence at the end of 1831 when war broke out between the two, Palmerston was unprepared. A year later Egyptian troops under Mehemet Ali's son Ibrahim were advancing into Asia Minor. In this desperate situation for the Turk, only the Russians were willing and able to act. Troops were sent to the Bosphorus and Russia stood revealed as Turkey's protector while, as Webster wrote, 'Britain . . . played a sorry part at Constantinople when the Sultan's throne hung in the balance'. Palmerston himself later described the failure of Britain to act on behalf of Turkey as 'that tremendous blunder of the English Government'. The result of

Russian assistance, which saved Asia Minor for the Sultan, was the mutual defence agreement of Unkiar Skelessi between Russia and Turkey, with a secret clause excusing Turkey her part provided she kept the Straits closed to warships of all nations. Palmerston, however, suspected something more sinister; that the Russians alone were empowered to move warships through the Straits. He saw the treaty as legalising a situation of 'protectorship' of Turkey by Russia, 'by which', he asserted, 'the Russian Ambassador becomes Chief Cabinet Minister of the Sultan'. Shocked by what he regarded as Russian expansionism, he was determined that Britain must not again be so passive in such an important matter, and worked to undo the particular relationship which Russia now apparently enjoyed.

Believing that the Tsar was bent upon the complete domination of Constantinople, Palmerston thought that this could be withstood better by support for the Sultan than for Mehemet Ali. If Mehemet Ali, whom Palmerston unlike some of his colleagues did not see as a genuine Westerniser and progressive, was to create a great Arab state, this must mean the collapse of the Turkish Empire and opportunity for Russian aggrandisement. He believed that Turkey was capable of modernisation and applauded the energetic, if ultimately totally unsuccessful attempts, of Mahmud to achieve it. Meanwhile he and Ponsonby, his ambassador at Constantinople, spared no effort to build up influence with the Turks. In this they were very successful, as shown by the advantageous commercial treaty of 1838.

Encouraged by his reforms and irked by the continued rule of Mehemet Ali over Syria despite British opposition, the Sultan determined to attack the Pasha in 1839, but suffered total defeat. Dying himself before news of the disaster reached him, he left a feeble youth as his successor to face a desperate situation. This crisis was somewhat similar to that of 1833, but now Palmerston acted with energy and incisiveness. He tried to organise a conference of ambassadors in London, but this was frustrated by Metternich. He then accepted a similar conference at Vienna, from which came the Collective Note of July 1839,which besought the Sultan to trust the Powers to maintain his Empire. The French government, however, disavowed the work of their ambassador and the Russian Tsar refused to continue the conference. In this situation Palmerston, holding to the Collective Note, decided that Britain must work through Russia. Whether what followed was partially a scheme of the Tsar's to break the British-French entente or the result of his realisation that Palmerston would not permit unilateral Russian action, is not certain, but what is sure is the enormous courage and perseverance of Palmerston in going against strong Cabinet opposition and mounting French threats to carry out the Collective Note's promises by co-operation with Russia.

What exactly France was trying to do in her support for Mehemet Ali is not easy to see. French involvement in Egypt was considerable but did not of itself demand assisting the Pasha in his aggrandisement. It seems that, jealous of Britain in the Mediterranean, Thiers and Louis Philippe desired a major diplomatic triumph in which French will should be seen to prevail over the other four Powers. Certainly France proved completely intransigent and gave the impression that she would go so far as to fight to maintain Mehemet Ali, whereas Britain and Russia wished, at the least, to drive him back into Egypt.

Sir Charles Webster has shown just how irresolute the Cabinet was in acting with Russia in opposition to France and how treacherous to Palmerston were such ministers as Lord Holland in passing on Cabinet secrets to the French to encourage their stand. At the same time Prussia and Austria were somewhat timid and had to be driven. Against all this and increasing French bellicosity, Palmerston, showing no sign of his worries, was resolute, while tireless in his efforts at persuading others. Believing that failure to act would leave the field to Russia, Palmerston threatened resignation—'If my judgement is wrong on this matter, it can be of little value upon any other'—and pressed ahead to secure in July 1840 two Conventions. These, excluding France, provided for assistance to the Sultan and laid down terms for Mehemet Ali which, if he did not accept, would leave the Sultan free to depose him. Doubts in the Cabinet, however, increased, with Russell now opposed to Palmerston, and it was still not certain how firm were the four Powers. In the event Palmerston was totally vindicated. British naval operations were successful after a cautious start and Ibrahim, his communications threatened and the seaboard under attack, was driven to retire upon Egypt. In all this France showed herself unwilling to go beyond bellicose language and Thiers was forced to resign. With Mehemet Ali penned back into Egypt in June 1841 the Straits Convention was signed – in which France joined. This put the closing of the Straits under collective guarantee of all the Powers, thus triumphantly reversing Unkiar Skelessi.

'The triumph of Palmerston in 1840 was perhaps the greatest which he ever won in his long connection with foreign affairs', wrote Webster; it certainly silenced his previous opponents. Some since, however, have remained critical, believing that Turkey was not really worth saving, that Russia was not the danger Palmerston feared and that friendship with France was a critical British interest. Nevertheless it would be wrong to judge the situation in 1839 by that of 1878, and it is difficult to see what stability there could have been in the area if Turkey had collapsed in 1839-40. Finally, it is difficult to follow the details of 1839-40 and still to blame Palmerston for ending the Franco-British entente.

As a concluding comment on Palmerston the blusterer, his own argument in favour of speaking out forcibly should be quoted. Many a case that is not urged goes by default and the subsequent situation becomes more serious because misunderstood. 'I am all for making a clatter against her [Russia]', Palmerston declared; 'depend upon it, that is the best way to save you from the necessity of making war against her.'

Chapter VI

Aberdeen and the Crimean War

1 The man and the Foreign Secretary Although twice Foreign Secretary (1828-30 and 1841-4) and Prime Minister (1852-5), the Earl of Aberdeen is surprisingly little known; one of the 'suppressed characters' of history, as his son claimed. Nevertheless, if unknown when compared to his two famous predecessors, Castlereagh and Canning, Aberdeen did share with them the early patronage and regard of William Pitt. Orphaned as a child, he turned to an old family friend, Dundas, and through Dundas he became well known to Pitt, subsequently spending most of his time at the houses of the two men. After leaving Cambridge Aberdeen travelled widely in Europe and the Near East; he pursued his well-developed archaeological and literary interests but also, because of his influential friends, he was able to meet distinguished people in the countries he visited.

Pitt's death in 1806 was a grievous blow to the young man, and he wrote, 'I have lost the only friend to whom I looked up with unbounded love and admiration.' It might have been expected to be a blow to his political aspirations as well, but he was offered and declined several official posts before he agreed to go as special envoy for Castlereagh to the Court of Austria. This post brought him into close contact with Metternich, and even if his trusting nature caused him at times to be deceived by the blandishments of the Austrian Chancellor, he was able to learn much about diplomacy. This period of his life also taught Aberdeen a horror of war, something he was never to lose.

Travelling in the wake of the Allied armies in their advance into France, he wrote of his feelings: 'The near approach of war and its effects, are horrible beyond what you can conceive ... the continual sight of the poor wounded wretches of all nations, haunts me night and day.' Nor was this just the conventional expression of fine sentiment. Aberdeen's dread of war is exemplified by the way he declined to restore a church on his estates near the end of his life because he felt his share in the Crimean War had disqualified him. He left the work to his son and quoted in explanation God's injunction to David: 'Thou hast shed blood abundantly, and hast made great wars; thou shalt not build an house unto my name, because thou hast shed much blood upon the earth in my sight.'

The Biblical precedent is typical of the man, for Aberdeen sought to apply Christian principles to his political life. In his diplomacy he showed moderation and tact, trying to take the charitable view of those with whom he dealt. He was, however, capable of firmness and determination as well as kindness. Gladstone commented: 'All the qualities and parts in which he was great were those that are the very foundation-stones of our being.'

After 1815 Aberdeen left public life—he was always a reluctant politician—and did not return until the Duke of Wellington formed his administration in 1828, soon becoming Foreign Secretary, an office he regained in Peel's government of 1841. With the break-up of the Conservative party following the repeal of the Corn Laws Aberdeen and Peel remained close colleagues. With Sir Robert's death, Aberdeen became the leader of the Peelites, and it was in this capacity that he became Prime Minister in the coalition which took office in 1852.

Aberdeen pursued the same policy in his two spells as Foreign Secretary, but was able to play a more positive role under Peel than under Wellington; Peel was less interested in foreign affairs than Wellington, and Aberdeen felt less need to defer to Peel, whom he saw more as an equal. Whenever possible he followed a policy of conciliation. This is revealed most clearly in his dealings with France, but also with Russia and the United States. Of Aberdeen's work in securing an entente with France after 1841 Algernon Cecil wrote: 'It was the great feather in Aberdeen's cap that . . . he recreated a good understanding which lasted during the six years of his administration, only to be lost again the moment Palmerston got back to power.' He was assisted by the two monarchs with their mutual visits and by his own cordial relations with Guizot, and was fortunate in being able to exploit the goodwill he had won earlier by persuading the Duke of Wellington to recognise Louis Philippe's assumption of the French throne in 1830. Nevertheless there was still considerable popular mistrust for any *rapprochement* on both sides of the Channel, and Aberdeen needed all his calm and tact to deal with such potential sources of trouble as rivalry over Tahiti and the question of future husbands for the Spanish Queen and her sister. Over the latter question Aberdeen went so far as to disavow the attempts of his ambassador at Madrid to steal a march on the French, and even reported to them the details of the intrigue. British rivalry with the United States over the Canadian frontier was also allayed by Aberdeen. 'This is an immense thing for the peace of the world', wrote Queen Victoria about his settlement of the disputes in Maine and Oregon.

In sharp contrast to Palmerston, Aberdeen resisted the notion that Britain should interfere in the affairs of other countries. He withdrew British troops from Portugal when he thought that they might become involved in civil war following Don Miguel's return, and he set his face against meddling in Spain or Greece. In 1844 he wrote to the British Minister at Athens to dissuade him from his attempts to influence the Greek government, 'The superior probity, enterprise, and wealth of British merchants will always ensure the preservation of British influence. I desire no other than that which arises from this source.' Sometimes this policy of non-interference has been construed as deliberately favouring despotism and reaction, but even if such was the outcome, it was not the objective.

Aberdeen was cautious, conciliatory and clear-sighted, and Cecil has asserted that 'if he were to be more fairly judged' he would be placed 'high upon the roll of British Foreign Secretaries'. However, Aberdeen's name—as Bright prophesied to him it would be—is remembered as that of the Prime Minister who presided over Britain's entrance into the only European war she fought between 1815 and 1914—the Crimean War.

2 The road to war In one sense the Crimean War is very easy to explain. Russo-Turkish rivalry was never very far from breaking out into open war from the eighteenth century onwards. By the late eighteenth century Britain had become alarmed enough at Russian expansion to the south-west to be extremely concerned at the prospect of such a war. When the wars occurred, (in the 1790s, the 1820s, the 1850s, and the 1870s) there was always a possibility that Britain might be drawn in to halt a Russian advance or to shore up a Turkish Empire which was near to final collapse. To this extent it is surprising not that Britain was drawn into war in 1854, but that this was the only such occasion.

Why did war break out between Russia and Turkey in 1853? One school of thought concentrates in its answer on Russian ambition—what Justin McCarthy, writing in the last century, referred to as 'the aggressive and aggrandising spirit of Russia'. That the Tsar was casting his eyes upon Turkey is proved by his conversations in 1853 with the British ambassador. He repeated the ideas he had put forward on his visit to England in 1844; of partition of the Turkish Empire, which was anyway about to die, and of the futility of attempted assistance. 'You may give him musk, but even musk will not long keep him alive.' Nicholas had before him a recent precedent of successful Austrian bullying of Turkey which presumably helped persuade him that the time for action had arrived. But also an immediate cause for dispute had arisen over the Holy Places in Palestine. In his attempts to pursue a forward policy and to win the support of the Catholics in France, Napoleon III had espoused the cause of the Latin Church in Palestine. The Latin Christians had increasingly lost control of the Holy Places to the Greeks, and Louis Napoleon now used French influence to demand restitution. Subsequent concessions to the Latins granted by the Turks at the expense of the Orthodox Christians angered the Tsar as the champion of the latter, and he used the supposed slight as the excuse for a diplomatic offensive.

Early in 1853 Prince Menshikov was despatched on a mission to Constantinople to seek satisfaction. His threatening stance and peremptory manner alarmed the British and French representatives and secured the replacement of a Turkish minister whom Menshikov believed to be particularly Russophobe. He then demanded that the Turks conclude a convention with Russia which, according to Temperley, 'implied a political as well as a religious protection, and carried with it the suggestion that Russia could interfere to enforce the guarantee'. With the Turkish refusal to accept the convention Menshikov departed from Constantinople, and by the end of May the Russians had decided to occupy the Danubian Principalities. This, it is claimed, was clearly the first step in a calculated Russian aggression.

After her troops had crossed into Moldavia on 3 July, however, Russia did not at once proceed to war with Turkey, and in the end it was Turkey who issued a declaration of war several months later. This apparent reluctance of the Russians to initiate hostilities has led some writers to question the view that the Russian Tsar wished to dismember Turkey. Perhaps Nicholas's reluctance is partly explained by his sudden realisation that Austria, despite the help he had given her in quelling revolt, was not going to be an ally in this crisis. Nevertheless Russia's inhibitions seem more deep-seated than this, and M. S. Anderson in *The Eastern Question* writes, 'Neither the Tsar nor his Foreign Minister wanted war . . . Nicholas stressed that it could help only the revolutionary forces in Europe.'

When in July the ambassadors of Britain, France and Prussia met the Austrian Foreign Minister in an endeavour to mediate between Russia and Turkey, the Tsar accepted the Vienna Note which embodied their proposals. Primarily these were that the Turks should observe the spirit of previous treaties with Russia and that they should make no change in the position of their

Christian subjects without consulting the Russian and French governments. It is true that Nesselrode, the Russian Foreign Minister, in his 'violent interpretation' subsequently claimed that this would give Russia the right to interfere in Turkey's affairs on behalf of the Christians in the Empire. This interpretation was later disavowed by the Tsar and it was, as already mentioned, the Turks who first attacked the Russians in the Principalities at the end of October, just as it was the Turks who sent the flotilla into the Black Sea which the Russians destroyed at Sinope on 30 November. Perhaps the answer is that Nicholas thought he could bully Turkey without having to contemplate war.

If the Russians were not seeking the destruction of the Ottoman Empire what did they want? A. J. P. Taylor in his *Struggle for the Mastery of Europe* writes: 'Their practical policy for the past twenty years had been the maintenance of the Ottoman Empire as a buffer state securing the Black Sea; the essential condition of this policy was that Turkey should fear Russia more than any other Power.' What had particularly alarmed the Tsar was Napoleon's bullying tactics, which threatened his position. Russia then was pursuing an essentially conservative policy towards Turkey. This argument is strengthened by the Tsar's identification of Napoleon with revolution. 'In his eyes', writes Taylor, '. . . the struggle between France and Russia was merely a cover for the far greater struggle between conservatism and "the revolution".' Hence Nicholas believed that Britain would never oppose him on such an issue.

Some historians have gone further and seen the crisis as deliberately provoked by Napoleon as a way of gaining an alliance with Britain and splitting her from Russia. 'If . . . we seek to find out who among mortals were most to blame, it seems that we must assign pre-eminence in responsibility to Napoleon III', wrote F. J. C. Hearnshaw in *The Cambridge History of British Foreign Policy*. This was to be the first step in a carefully planned policy of breaking up the coalition which had defeated his uncle, and the start of an alliance of peoples against kings. Although Louis Napoleon clearly did wish for an alliance with Britain and was seeking to pursue a forward policy, the Napoleonic plot theory is hardly substantiated by the doubts and heart-searchings which accompanied nearly all of his moves throughout the crisis.

Another explanation points to the British ambassador at Constantinople as the man responsible for war. Stratford Canning had already been ambassador to the Sultan on more than one occasion when he returned to Constantinople at the request of the British government in 1853. His detractors see him as one who, using his great influence with the Turks and at times secretly going against his government's policy, set out to steel Turkey's will to war with Russia. Sometimes it is claimed that Stratford was passionately anti-Russian on personal grounds, from the time when the Tsar had refused to accept him as British ambassador at St. Petersburg in 1832. A less fanciful suggestion holds that he believed Russia a danger to Britain and pursued a policy of humbling her. John Morley, in his biography of Gladstone, claimed: 'Another obstacle to a pacific solution, perhaps most formidable of them all, was Lord Stratford de Redcliffe.' Several writers have quoted the British Foreign Secretary Clarendon, talking of Stratford: 'The titular Sultan is for peace but the real Sultan thinks now or never is the time for putting an end to Russia.' He is specifically seen as responsible for persuading Turkey to resist the Menshikov demands and later for refusing the Vienna Note as well as maintaining a continual barrage of anti-Russian propaganda.

Harold Temperley, however, in his *England and the Near East* has attacked this view. He claims that Stratford did all that he could to persuade the Turks to conciliate Menshikov and to accept the Vienna Note, even to drafting another set of proposals which he believed that the Turks and the Russians would be able to accept. He strove to dissuade the Sultan from declaring war against Russia, and for several weeks he ignored his government's order to summon the British fleet to Constantinople in an attempt to damp down antagonisms. The comments of ministers which blame Stratford Canning are described by A. J. P. Taylor as 'the irritation' of men in a 'state of muddle and hesitation against the man who presented the issues clearly and without pretence'. Nevertheless some doubt remains as to what Stratford told the Turks unofficially, and it is true that his very presence, bearing in mind his reputation, seemed to confirm British support for the Turks. However, when all is said Turkish hostility to Russia can easily be explained as their natural fury at what seemed aggressive and bullying policy. It has often been argued that British policy, or lack of it, allowed the Russo-Turkish war to occur and then failed to prevent Britain from being dragged into it. On the one hand a firmer British stand, the Palmerston-Russell policy, would have made it clear to Russia from the outset that Britain would not tolerate any interference with Turkey and would have dissuaded the Tsar from embarking on such policies. On the other hand, it is claimed, if Britain had been more determined with Turkey, showing that she was not prepared to assist her against Russia, the Sultan would have been more ready for compromise. The dilemma is revealed in Aberdeen himself, who thoroughly disliked the idea of assisting the Turks to maintain their empire, especially when this meant harsh misrule over Christians, but at the same time was alive to the dangers of Russian advance in the Near East since 1828. In fact Aberdeen's dislike of Turkish rule coupled with his abhorrence of war meant that he did not support Turkey but tried to bring pressure upon her to settle with Russia. In the event of war Russian success might reasonably have been confined to certain acceptable limits which the other Great Powers could have stipulated, on the lines of what happened in the 1820s and the 1870s. It should, however, be remembered that in the 1850s there was no Continental statesman of the ability and prestige of a Bismarck or a Metternich to concert the Powers against Russian aggrandisement.

Aberdeen, however, was not able to pursue this policy throughout. One important reason was that influential members of his Cabinet held contrary views. Palmerston and Russell both believed that Russia must be firmly resisted and that the onset of war between Turkey and Russia merely made such resistance more necessary. In Russell's words, 'The question must be decided by war, and if we do not stop the Russians on the Danube, we shall have to stop them on the Indus.' Not only was it that Palmerston and Russell were strong personalities in the Cabinet; the Cabinet was a coalition and liable to split anyway. (Palmerston did in fact resign in December 1853 on a disagreement primarily over parliamentary reform but which included differences arising from the Eastern Question; however, he returned within ten days.) No Cabinet can have contained so many Foreign Secretaries; Aberdeen, Russell, Palmerston, Granville and Clarendon had all occupied the office, and this in itself was hardly likely to make for unanimity in foreign policy.

However uncertain the Government was, public opinion was adamant. One writer claimed, 'The war was regretted by the government and demanded by the people', and another has stressed 'weakness in Downing Street—and emotion in Fleet Street'. The Press in particular lambasted the government for its pusillanimity in not standing up to the Russians. Greville wrote at the time: 'Day after day the Radical and Tory papers, animated by very different sentiments and motives, pour forth the most virulent abuse of the Emperor of Russia, of Austria and of the Government, especially of Aberdeen.' The government and Prince Albert were seen as being in the pay of the Russians, and when a Turkish flotilla cruising in the Black Sea was sunk at Sinope by the Russians, public opinion became almost hysterical. It is not surprising that a divided Cabinet should find it increasingly difficult to resist popular demand.

Clarendon, the current Foreign Secretary, pursued Aberdeen's policy, but a little less enthusiastically than his leader. Because of his need to hold his Cabinet together, Aberdeen found himself moving step by step towards support of Turkey. Clarendon moved faster and less reluctantly in the same direction, making it harder for the Prime Minister to hold out. For instance, after the violent interpretation by Nesselrode of the Vienna Note, Clarendon became much more anti-Russian. Some have seen this as sincere and claim that he had come to distrust the Tsar's motives; others argue that it merely provided the excuse to espouse a more popular policy. The Government thus consented to the fleet moving to Besika Bay in June 1853, and at the end of September, with rioting in Constantinople, the fleet was ordered there, an order that was repeated more urgently in early October. After the battle of Sinope the Cabinet agreed that British ships should co-operate with the French in blockading the Russian navy in Sebastopol and act generally to protect Turkey in the Black Sea. Finally an ultimatum was issued, demanding a Russian withdrawal from the Principalities, and when it was not complied with war was declared on 27 March 1854.

One reason, some would stress it as the main reason, for hostility to Russia was resentment at the manner in which the Tsar had stood against revolution in 1848-9 and in particular at his crushing of the Hungarian revolt. Justin McCarthy wrote in 1881 that it became 'a fixed conviction in the mind of Liberalism in Western Europe that Russia was the greatest obstacle . . . to the spread of popular ideas'. Similarly L. C. B. Seaman believes 'the Crimean War was based not so much on the Eastern Question as on the ideological breach between East and West first made manifest at Troppau'.

Of course those who subscribe to the theory that the war was begun by Louis Napoleon would accept this notion of an ideological conflict. However, those who see Russia as the arch-aggressor bent on extending her territory reject such a concept. Tennyson at the time, and A. W. Kinglake writing later in the century, both saw in anti-Russian feeling and the thirst for strong measures the process of Britain at last waking up to her obligations and casting off her lethargy and timidity. Tennyson wrote in *Maud*:

> . . . so I wake to the higher aims
> Of a land that has lost for a little her lust of gold,
> And love of a peace that was full of wrongs and shames.

Kinglake believed that the British fashion for the pursuit of material wealth and the decrying of military virtue had contributed to Russian self-confidence.

Surveying the whole European background of the war most modern writers have concentrated upon the weakness and indecision of the various governments—'nerveless confusion which led to the substitution of general hysteria for confident diplomacy'. Nicholas is said to have misread the minds of the other Powers, to have blundered in using Menshikov and to have been too proud to back down. Louis Napoleon vaguely pursued a forward policy and wished to retain British friendship; he also was frightened to back down as the quarrel developed. Austria did not know what policy to pursue, not wanting to quarrel with Russia but opposed to her aggressive designs on Turkey. Prussia had no Near Eastern policy but was restive at merely following Austria's lead. Britain dithered between neutrality and involvement and finally, with a coalition government pushed forward by public opinion, tried for a compromise and got the worst of both policies. M. S. Anderson expresses this view very clearly: 'The Crimean War was thus the outcome of a series of misjudgements, misunderstandings and blunders, of stupidity, pride and obstinacy rather than of ill will. More than any great war of modern times, it took place by accident.' If this is a fair picture then clearly Aberdeen must shoulder a considerable share of the blame for the war, with what Asa Briggs has called his 'good-natured ineptitude'. On the other hand it can be argued that he exhausted every opportunity for peace, which some of his colleagues would not have done. He himself considered afterwards that it was a just war but implied that it was unnecessary. However laudable the reasons for his lack of bellicosity and however understandable his final deference to his Cabinet, the decisions of his government were finally his responsibility.

A. J. P. Taylor, while not dismissing much of the above and paying particular attention to Louis Napoleon's share in the conflict, shows, somewhat characteristically, to what extent political leaders were mastered by practicabilities. For instance the fleets, having been sent to Besika Bay, could not be left there over the winter, and in the absence of any Russian concession the only possibilities were a retreat or a forward move, such as to Constantinople.

At the time Cobden and Bright both opposed the war, refusing to see it as just or in Britain's interests, political or commercial. However, one historian, V. J. Puryear, has stressed that Britain's growing trading interest in the Black Sea area and the more favourable commercial policies of the Turks naturally inclined Britain to Turkey's side, but this has not been a widely accepted point of view.

3 **The war and its results**   The course of the war was drasti-
cally altered almost at the outset when, under Austrian demands,
the Russians withdrew from the Principalities. At once the allied
plans for an advance through the Principalities became impossible,
and instead the troops were embarked from Varna and used in an
invasion of the Crimean Peninsula with the aim of eliminating
Russian power in the Black Sea. The expedition, considering the
inadequate planning and woeful liaison between the allies, came
surprisingly near to success, and Sebastopol might have fallen by
late autumn. As it was, timid leadership allowed the chance to slip
and the war settled down into stalemate. Tsar Nicholas died and
was succeeded by Alexander II, the allies were joined by Sardinia-
Piedmont, Sebastopol at last fell, but peace seemed little nearer.
The bleak prospect provoked Louis Napoleon's demand that the
war be ended or widened, with such aims as the reconstitution of
Poland. Finally, however, it was the Austrian ultimatum to Russia
in December 1855 which forced the Tsar to accept the allied peace
terms. The settlement was concluded at the Conference of Paris
and embodied in treaty form at the end of March.

The peace had three important features. First, the Black Sea
was to be open to all trading vessels and closed to all warships, a
neutrality that extended to the prohibition of naval stores and
bases on the coastline. Although this applied also to the Turks it was
the Russians, as the stronger power, who suffered a real humiliation in the "Black Sea Clause". Secondly Turkey was not invited
to 'share in the advantages of the European Concert' and the
Powers pledged her integrity, while the Sultan promised better
treatment for his Christian subjects. Thirdly the Danubian
Principalities were freed from Russian tutelage and given an
autonomy under nominal Turkish sovereignty which was guaranteed by the Powers.

Leaving aside its domestic effects, what did the Crimean War
achieve for Britain, and did the results have any relation to the
causes for which it was fought? If the war was fought to sustain
the Ottoman Empire and preserve her independence it was, in the
long run, clearly a failure. Turkey had been protected, but was no
stronger and no better able to look after herself. Reform did not

follow, and in fact the Sultan became less responsive to pressure for change, believing himself secured by the rivalries of the Powers.

Russia had suffered a defeat, but there is dispute about its extent. Many writers have concentrated upon Russia's success in abrogating the "Black Sea Clause" in 1870 and her renewed attack upon Turkey in 1877, pointing to these as evidence for the failure of Britain to administer a decisive check. The nature of the operations would anyhow have prevented a calamitous defeat, but some historians recently have claimed that Russia's defeat was nevertheless substantial. A. J. P. Taylor writes: 'The war shattered both the myth and the reality of Russian power ... After 1856 Russia carried less weight in European affairs than at any time since the end of the Great Northern War in 1721; and the predominance which she had exercised at Berlin and Vienna before 1854 she was never to wield again until 1945.' In this respect the defeat of Russia, if not necessarily in the British national interest, was in accord with the wishes of those who had opposed the Tsar as, in the words of Tocqueville, 'the corner-stone of despotism in the world'.

Whatever the wishes of the British people, it was far from the aim of the British Government of 1854 to raise Louis Napoleon to the summit of his international reputation in the short term, and in the longer term to create a fluidity in international affairs which had not existed since 1815, and which allowed the outbreak of three major European wars and the creation of two major European states, all in the space of fifteen years. This, the dawn of a new era in European relations, assuredly was not why Britain had embarked on the invasion of the Crimea.

Chronological table of events

1789 Meeting of Estates-General in France
1793 Execution of French King. Britain and France at war
1799 Consulate in France with Napoleon as First Consul
1802 Peace of Amiens
1803 War between Britain and France resumed
1804 Napoleon declared Emperor
1812 Napoleon's Russian campaign. War between Britain and U.S.A.
1813 Napoleon defeated at Leipzig
1814 Treaty of Chaumont. First Peace of Paris. Congress of Vienna opens. French monarchy restored
1815 Napoleon defeated at Waterloo. Holy Alliance signed. Second Peace of Paris. Quadruple Alliance
1818 Congress of Aix-la-Chapelle
1820-1 Revolts in Spain, Italy and Greece. Congress of Troppau (1820); reconvened at Laibach (1821)
1822 Congress of Verona
1823 French troops invade Spain
1825 Death (December) of Alexander I. Nicholas I becomes Tsar of Russia
1827 Battle of Navarino
1828-9 War between Russia and Turkey
1830 Revolutions in France, Belgium, Poland and Germany
1831 Revolution in Italy. War between Ottoman Sultan and Mehemet Ali
1833 Treaty of Unkiar Skelessi between Turkey and Russia
1834 Quadruple Alliance—Britain, France, Spain and Portugal
1839 War between Sultan and Mehemet Ali
1841 Straits Convention signed
1846 Pius IX becomes Pope. Affair of the Spanish Marriages
1847 Civil war in Switzerland
1848 "Year of Revolutions". Fall of monarchy in France. Fall of Metternich. Louis Napoleon becomes President of Second Republic
1849 Revolutions in Italy and Hungary defeated
1851 Louis Napoleon's *coup d'état*
1852 Louis Napoleon becomes Emperor
1853 War between Russia and Turkey
1854 Crimean War begins
1855 Alexander II succeeds Nicholas I as Tsar
1856 Crimean War ends. Paris Peace Conference
1858 Orsini's attempt to assassinate Louis Napoleon
1859 France and Piedmont at war with Austria
1860 Garibaldi's campaign in Sicily and Naples
1861 Kingdom of Italy proclaimed (Venice and Rome remain outside) Civil war begins in U.S.A.
1863 Revolt of Poles
1864 War over Schleswig-Holstein; Prussia and Austria invade Denmark
1865 Civil war in U.S.A. ends
1866 Austro-Prussian war

Ministries

MINISTRY FORMED	PRIME MINISTER	FOREIGN SECRETARY
June 1812	Lord Liverpool	**Viscount Castlereagh** from 1822—**Canning**
April 1827	**George Canning**	Earl of Dudley
September 1827	Viscount Goderich	Earl of Dudley
January 1828	Duke of Wellington	Earl of Dudley May 1828—**Aberdeen**
November 1830	Earl Grey	**Viscount Palmerston**
July 1834	Viscount Melbourne	**Viscount Palmerston**
December 1834	Sir Robert Peel	Duke of Wellington
March 1835	Viscount Melbourne	**Viscount Palmerston**
September 1841	Sir Robert Peel	**Earl of Aberdeen**
July 1846	Earl Russell	**Viscount Palmerston** from 1851—Granville
February 1852	Earl of Derby	Earl of Malmesbury
December 1852	**Earl of Aberdeen**	Earl Russell from 1853—Clarendon
February 1855	**Viscount Palmerston**	Earl of Clarendon
February 1858	Earl of Derby	Earl of Malmesbury
June 1859	**Viscount Palmerston**	Earl Russell
October 1865	Earl Russell	Earl of Clarendon

Monarchs

1760-1820 George III (George, Prince of Wales—Regent 1811-1820)
1820-1830 George IV
1830-1837 William IV
1837-1901 Victoria

Further reading

Space permits mention of only the most important and readable books. Those wishing to examine particular aspects in detail should consult the bibliographies included in the works listed below. The list is divided into two sections: I. Works of interest for much or all of the period covered. II. Works which deal with a particular Foreign Secretary or period.

I

Albrecht-Carrie, R. *A Diplomatic History of Europe since 1815*, 1958

Anderson, M. S., *The Eastern Question*, 1966. (Sound and full of information; presents the results of the bulk of recent research)

Bartlett, C. J. (Ed.) *Britain Pre-eminent*, 1969. (A very useful and stimulating collection of essays on the period)

Cecil, A. *British Foreign Secretaries 1807-1916*, 1927. (Covers all the Foreign Secretaries and, although a little uncritical, extremely helpful on less well-known figures)

Joll, J. (Ed.) *Britain and Europe 1793-1916*, 1950. (Useful documents and a stimulating introduction)

Seaman, L. C. B. *From Vienna to Versailles*, 1955. (European rather than British. Although sometimes outrageous, it is very lively and challenges some accepted doctrines)

Seton-Watson, R. W. *Britain in Europe 1789-1814*, 1937. (A very useful standard account of British foreign policy)

Taylor, A. J. P. *The Struggle for Mastery in Europe 1848-1918*, 1954. (Again European rather than centred on Britain, but first class and with some very helpful chapters)

Temperley, H. & Penson, L. M. *Foundations of British Foreign Policy*, 1938. (Invaluable as a source of documents)

Ward, Sir A. W. & Gooch, G. P. (Eds.) *Cambridge History of British Foreign Policy, Volume II 1815-1866*, 1923. (Rather uneven and some chapters a little dated, but still useful)

II

Castlereagh

Bartlett, C. J. *Castlereagh*, 1966. (Recent biography; clear and reasonable, if orthodox, account)

Leigh, Iona. *Castlereagh*. (A readable biography)

Montgomery Hyde, H. *The Strange Death of Lord Castlereagh*, 1959. (Fascinating attempt to reconstruct his collapse, by an authority on Castlereagh's early life)

Webster, Sir C. K. *The Foreign Policy of Castlereagh 1812-1815*, 1932 and *The Foreign Policy of Castlereagh 1815-1822*, 1934. (Still the essential starting point for any detailed work on his foreign policy)

Canning

Rolo, P. J. V. *George Canning: Three Biographical Studies*, 1965. (A very interesting and helpful work)

Temperley, H. W. V. *The Foreign Policy of Canning, 1822-1827*, 1925. (Essential reading, if a little laudatory)

Palmerston

Ayling, S. E. *Nineteenth Century Gallery*. (Has a useful chapter on Palmerston)

Pemberton, W. B. *Lord Palmerston*. (A readable biography)

Ridley, J. *Lord Palmerston*, 1970. (Recent biography, very full and interesting; does not offer any new interpretations of his foreign policy)

Southgate, D. *"The Most English Minister": the policies and politics of Palmerston*, 1965. (At times very shrewd and helpful; not entirely satisfactory)

Webster, Sir C. K. *The Foreign Policy of Palmerston, 1830-1841*, 2 vols., 1951. (First class)

The Vienna Settlement and the Restoration Period

Kissinger, H. *A World Restored*, 1947. (Particularly favourable to Metternich: an interesting book)

Nicolson, Sir H. *The Congress of Vienna. A Study in Allied Unity, 1812-1822*, 1946. (Lively and entertaining although less good on the post-Vienna period)

Webster, Sir C. K. *The Congress of Vienna, 1814-1815*, 1919. (Shorter, more factual and specific, but less lively)

The Greek Revolt and the Crimean War

Henderson, G. B. *Crimean War Diplomacy and other Historical Essays*, 1947. (Very useful indeed)

Index